Fishing New England
A Cape Cod Shore Guide

About the Author

Gene Bourque, editor of *On The Water* magazine, grew up in Mystic, Connecticut, across the river from the Mystic Seaport. He moved to Falmouth, Massachusetts, in 1973, and fell in love with the beaches, jetties, estuaries and rips of Cape Cod and the Islands from Cuttyhunk to Provincetown. He has worked in tackle shops on the Cape, taught fly-fishing and fly-tying, has been a shore guide, and gives seminars on Cape Cod fishing techniques and locations for fishing clubs and at outdoor sporting shows throughout the Northeast. He was a contributing writer to *On The Water* before joining the staff in 1999.

Fishing New England

A Cape Cod Shore Guide

by Gene Bourque

On The Water
Falmouth, MA

Printed in the United States of America

Library of Congress Card Number: 00-110739

ISBN # 0-9706538-0-8

10 9 8 7 6 5 4 3 2 1

Book design by Joanne M. Briana-Gartner
Cover photograph by Brenda Sharp
Interior photographs by: Gene Bourque, Brenda Sharp, Amy Hamilton,
Joanne Briana-Gartner, Erik Oliver, John Burke, Bill LaPierre and Erin Healy

Dedication

To my father, Warren Bourque, who loved the ocean, wooden boats, and taught me that catching fish was really not the most important part of going fishing.

Contents

Preface

Sometime around the first week of April the rumors will start in the local tackle shops. Someone hears that someone caught a striper in one of the local estuaries or perhaps off South Cape or Popponesset beaches in Mashpee. The reporter of this rumor will swear that the alleged fish was dark and healthy looking, not the thin, pale stripers that hold over in some of the rivers and salt marshes.

This rumor will spread quickly and in spite of cold, damp weather and cutting wind, cars and trucks with fishing rods on their roofs will appear in beach parking lots and along back roads near the south shore of the Cape. Anglers will debate how the past winter's weather will affect the striper's arrival after migrating from the Hudson River, Delaware Bay and Chesapeake Bay. If the past winter was relatively mild, some fishermen will be convinced that the rumor is true, that the water must be warmer than usual, and that the first bass must be around. And so they'll rig up and head for the water to cast for an hour or so.

Even if it's a warm day, the water temperature will still be in the low 40s, and if the wind is blowing, fingers and hands soon become numb. The hardcore striper addicts all know that the chances are slim to none that they'll hook up, but still they stand at the shore and cast spinning, conventional or fly rods until the cold drives them to their cars for a hot thermos of coffee. No fish have been caught, but the season has begun.

In years past when small stripers could be kept legally, many tackle shops ran "first striper of the season" contests. The angler who weighed in the first fish was guaranteed a certain amount of local celebrity status, cash prizes or free tackle and his or her picture in the local paper. This first fish was always caught in the middle or toward the end of April. Of course, these were always small fish, 16 or 18 inches, weighing a couple of pounds, because these are the first fish to show up along the Cape. These small fish seem to fight surprisingly well on light tackle, or maybe any bend in the fishing rod feels good after a long winter.

Coinciding with the arrival of the first

schoolies is the start of the spring herring run. Some years scouts show up in the runs as early as February, but the majority of the fish start up the coastal streams in early April, with the run peaking in mid-May. The heaviest concentration of these fish signals the local fishermen to start looking for larger stripers. Elaborate holding tanks called livewells are constructed in the backs of pickup trucks or even in car trunks, aerated by pumps connected to the vehicle's battery. This is crucial because the herring and their cousins, the alewives, die quickly in water that isn't heavily oxygenated, and lively herring are thought to be the absolute best early-season striper bait. In the dead of night anglers net herring in the runs and drive to the Cape Cod Canal or load the silvery baitfish into tanks onto boats to be fished in Woods Hole.

The first keeper, or legal-sized fish, usually comes from one of these locations, but the exact spot where the fish was caught will be a closely guarded secret. The largest stripers seem to arrive just as the herring are becoming scarce and some Cape fishermen keep dozens or even hundreds of the baitfish in pens called livecars, suspended off local docks. Some even resort to keeping the herring in children's swimming pools in their basements, a testament to the value of these small fish in May and June.

A generation ago another rite of spring was

winter flounder fishing at the mouths of estuaries and salt ponds. The flatfish would emerge from the mud as the water warmed in March and April, and every bridge on the Cape would be lined with anglers bouncing weights and hooks on the bottom, baited with seaworms, hoping to catch a few of the tasty fish. This fishery had many devotees, a credit to the flounder's abundance and status as superior table fare, if not its fighting abilities. There was also a social aspect to flounder fishing, with whole families involved, standing shoulder to shoulder in popular spots and catching fish after a long winter confined indoors.

Unfortunately, the flounder's popularity as a food fish led to overfishing of the species, both by recreational anglers and commercial anglers. Another factor in the flounder's demise was the degradation of the salt ponds. As nutrient levels changed with the use of lawn chemicals and salt run-off from coastal roads, eelgrass died and algae grew, raising water temperatures and lowering oxygen levels. Tens of thousands of baby flounder died every summer and soon the flounder fishing of the spring and fall was a thing of the past.

For many anglers in the Northeast, the first real sport-fishing experience of their lives happens compliments of another seasonal visitor, the bluefish. Showing up every year in mid or late May, first at South Cape Beach or Popponesset in Mashpee, these voracious fighters will hit just about any surface or subsurface lure. A fisherman will soon find out the importance of fresh line and a well-lubed reel with new drag washers when the choppers arrive. These first fish of the season will be long, lean racers, fish that will weigh 6 to 10 pounds, but be half again as heavy in a few weeks. Fishermen who have had to be content with catch-and-release striper fishing will now get to take a fish or two home for supper or the neighbor's table. In spite of a reputation as a strong, oily tasting fish, Cape fishermen know that a freshly caught, bled and iced bluefish is delicious.

By June sport fishing is in full swing on the Cape. Schools of small striped bass can be found in harbors, estuaries and rivers. Bigger stripers and bluefish are being caught along the outer beaches, near herring runs and in the Cape Cod Canal. Fluke (summer flounder), scup, tautog and black sea bass keep bottom fishers happy. Even though summer is just around the corner, it's still possible to find a parking spot at the beaches. The water is warming rapidly, baitfish are active and abundant, and the days are long. Many Cape anglers will say that June is their favorite month of the year.

The crowds descend on Cape Cod in July and many of these visitors come to the Cape to fish. Popular and well-known fishing spots can be crowded, so the smart fisher will seek out locations that are a little off the beaten path. It is in July that local shore fishermen will spend more time fishing after sunset and just before sunrise. This is to avoid crowds, but it's also when stripers feed actively in the rapidly warming water.

On the Cape Cod Bay side, the water remains cooler and the sand flats off Wellfleet, Brewster and Barnstable Harbor are filled with sand eels. Stripers can be seen cruising over the clear sand in very shallow water, feeding on these thin baitfish. Light-tackle enthusiasts and fly-fishers who wade and sight-cast here compare this fishery to bonefishing in the Bahamas.

Along the south shore of the Cape, anglers will be on the lookout for the next visitor from

southern waters, the bonito. The shore-bound fisher is at a distinct disadvantage compared to his brethren in boats when trying to hook-up with these speedy fish, but small schools of bonito do occasionally swing in close to shore. Light tackle is the rule and these small members of the tuna family, which can easily empty a reel, win new devotees every year.

The heat of August slows down the striper fishing, but other species make their way into Cape Cod waters. Spanish mackerel and false albacore are found in the same areas frequented by bonito, and a few anglers will score a Cape Cod grand slam: a striper, bluefish, false albacore and bonito caught on the same day. Schools of menhaden, or pogies, will be migrating along the coast and into harbors, followed closely by big bluefish. Every year a few exotic fish are caught on the Cape or just offshore in August, fish like cobia, wahoo and jacks. A small but dedicated group of shore anglers target brown sharks, bait-fishing off the southside beaches after dark with heavy conventional gear and catching specimens to 150 pounds.

Starting right after Labor Day and continuing through October the beaches from Chatham to Provincetown feature some of the best striped bass fishing in the world. Casting eels after dark or retrieving swimming plugs in the big surf, there is a very real possibility of catching a striper that weighs 40 pounds or more. Big bluefish cruise these beaches, too, sometimes chasing schools of menhaden or spike mackerel up onto the beach.

This is challenging fishing; the shifting sandbars change yearly or even after a severe storm and experienced anglers spend as much time scouting locations as actually fishing. The water can be dirty with a fine, clinging seaweed called mung, making fishing impossible. Although large fish are taken during the day, this remains primarily a nighttime fishery and striper addicts learn to sleep all day and fish all night. Race Point and Herring Cove in Provincetown are the destinations of surf-fishing enthusiasts from throughout the Northeast hoping for the striper of a lifetime.

Along the banks of the Canal, the fall

migration of striped bass is also anticipated. After a spring and summer of using live or chunked bait, Canal regulars welcome fall days when large popping plugs out-fish just about anything else. Many of the wooden lures that are found in every striper fisherman's tackle box were invented for Canal fishing.

There is a certain desperation to fishing at this time of year. The stripers and bluefish will soon be gone for the year, and every moment of fishing time becomes more valuable. The weather can be glorious one day and a northeast coastal storm can blow in the next. Fishermen are more willing to endure long, cold nights on the beach, knowing that there will be plenty of time to sit and be warm at home in the months to come. The water changes from blue to a steely gray, and the terns, which have guided fishermen to the fish all summer, disappear. There is more of an adversarial relationship between the angler and not just his quarry, but the environment itself. The water is colder, the air is colder, the fish fight harder, and the angler must be prepared for all these things.

In spite of this, there will still be cars with fishing rods on their roofs driving the shore roads and idling in beach parking lots until Thanksgiving, even though the migration has passed. Because someone told someone that a nice fish was caught off the beach somewhere just the other day.

Acknowledgements

Special thanks go to the following anglers, experts all, who suggested locations to be included in this book or provided valuable insights into the history, techniques and lore of Cape Cod fishing: Jim Young, Dave Laporte, Paul Newmier, Steve Shiraka, Tony Stetzko, Dave Peros, Art Crago, Alan Cordts, Jeffrey Joiner, Mike Arritt, and the crew at *On The Water*.

Introduction

Experienced fishermen tend to be a tight-lipped group, nowhere more so than on Cape Cod. Information is given grudgingly, even at many tackle shops where business depends on customers catching fish. Secrets about fishing methods and locations are usually handed down only after the recipient is deemed worthy, judged by the amount of time spent on the water and the passion for the sport. Some secrets are never revealed, only to be rediscovered by a new generation of anglers. Should this attitude be chalked up to the need to be "high hook," over-protective in nature, or just plain old Yankee crankiness? Maybe it's a little of each.

With the resurgence of striped bass stocks in recent years, more people than ever are taking up sport fishing. The purpose of this book is to guide and inform the reader by suggested fishing locations, explain techniques used to catch different species of sport fish and give historical perspective to the rich tradition of Cape Cod fishing. There are no deep, dark secrets here, although some spots are less known than others. It is hoped that the reader will use this book as a reference, but also as a wish list, because every fisherman knows that anticipating a fishing trip is almost as much fun as the trip itself.

The criteria used to determine if a location should be included in this book were quite simple: Does the angler have a better-than-average chance of finding fish at this location? And, is there public access and parking nearby? It's no exaggeration to say that the entire shoreline of Cape Cod will have sport fish nearby at some point during the fishing season. But certain spots feature the combination of a dependable food source, good cover and the right tidal conditions, year after year. These spots will usually hold fish when other spots are barren.

The population of the Cape has grown tremendously in the last 20 years, and with this growth has come greater limits to public access to the shore. Prime shorefront real estate is being purchased for astronomical sums of money and the new owners often restrict or deny access to prime fishing locations. Federal and state laws guarantee fishing rights in the inter-tidal, or "wet sand," zone along the entire shore line but the angler must not cross private property to get there. Every location included in this book is accessible by the public. In some cases, a certain amount of effort is involved to get to the prime areas, but a longer walk usually means fewer fishermen will share the spot.

There's an old adage in fishing circles, "That's why they call it fishing, not catching!" This sums up what to expect from this book. The spots and techniques outlined here are offered with the understanding that there is no such thing as an absolute, never-fail fishing location or method. The purpose here is to make the angler's time spent on the water more rewarding, secure in the knowledge that they are in a good spot, using proven techniques.

Gene Bourque

Access Information

Because Cape Cod is one of the premier summer vacation destinations in the United States, beach access and parking regulations are more restrictive at the height of the tourist season in many of the towns listed. These restrictions can change year to year in some locations, depending on expected use and such variables as damage from winter storms, improvements made to the area to accommodate increased use, and state or federal restrictions due to the presence of nesting birds.

Fishermen should expect to pay to park at many of the beaches listed in this book, especially if they arrive during daylight hours or plan to park within the boundaries of the Cape Cod National Seashore. Although most town, state and federal beach areas are free of fees and most restrictions in the off season, it is recommended that fishermen call the agencies listed below for specific information. This is especially important for fishermen intending to drive four-wheel-drive vehicles on the beach.

Cape Cod National Seashore
Salt Pond Visitor's Center, Eastham
(508) 255-3421
Seashore Permit Information
(508) 349-3785 extension 214

Bourne – Department of Natural Resources
(508) 759-0623

Falmouth – Beach Committee
(508) 548-8623

Mashpee
Town Hall, Leisure Services Department
(508) 539-1400 extension 519

Sandwich – Recreation Department
(508) 888-4361

Barnstable/Hyannis
Recreation Department
(508) 790-6345

Yarmouth – Parks Department
(508) 775-7910

Dennis – Beach/Harbormaster's Office
(508) 760-6159

Brewster – Recreation Department
(508) 896-9430

Harwich – Recreation Department
(508) 430-7553

Chatham – Recreation Center
(508) 945-5175

Orleans – Park Commission, Nauset Beach
(508) 240-3780

Eastham – Beach and Recreation Department
(508) 240-5974

Wellfleet – Beach Sticker Office
(508) 349-9818

Truro – Beach Commission (seasonal)
(508) 349-3939

Provincetown – Recreation Department
(508) 487-7097

Cape Cod

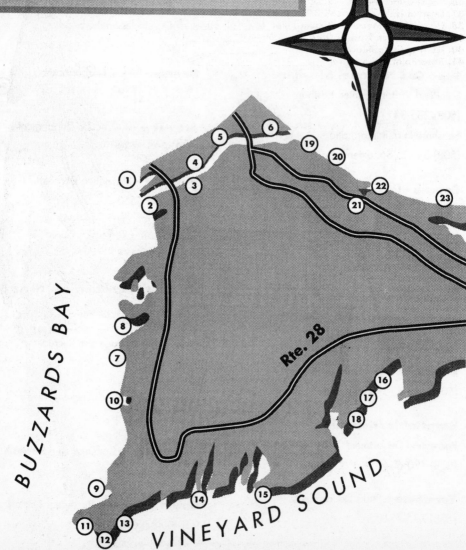

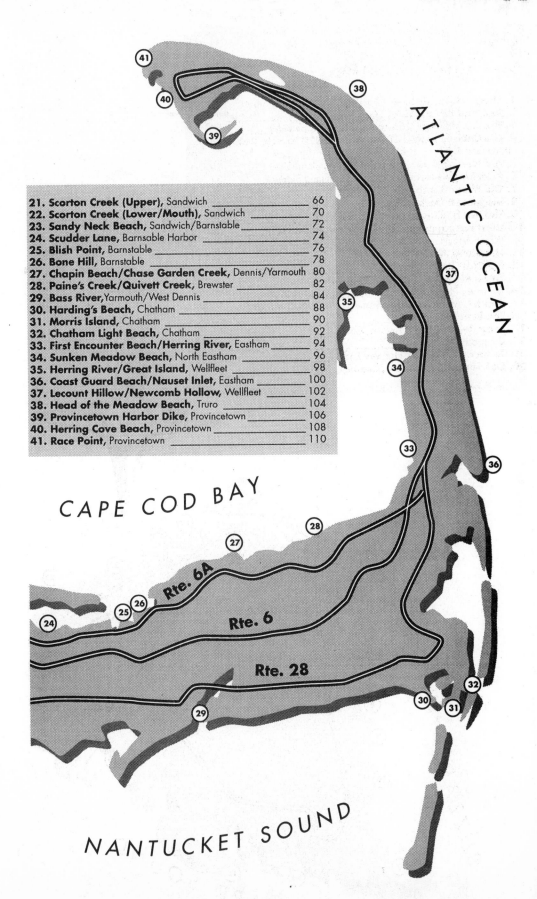

ATLANTIC OCEAN

CAPE COD BAY

Rte. 6A

Rte. 6

Rte. 28

NANTUCKET SOUND

Fishing New England

A Cape Cod Shore Guide

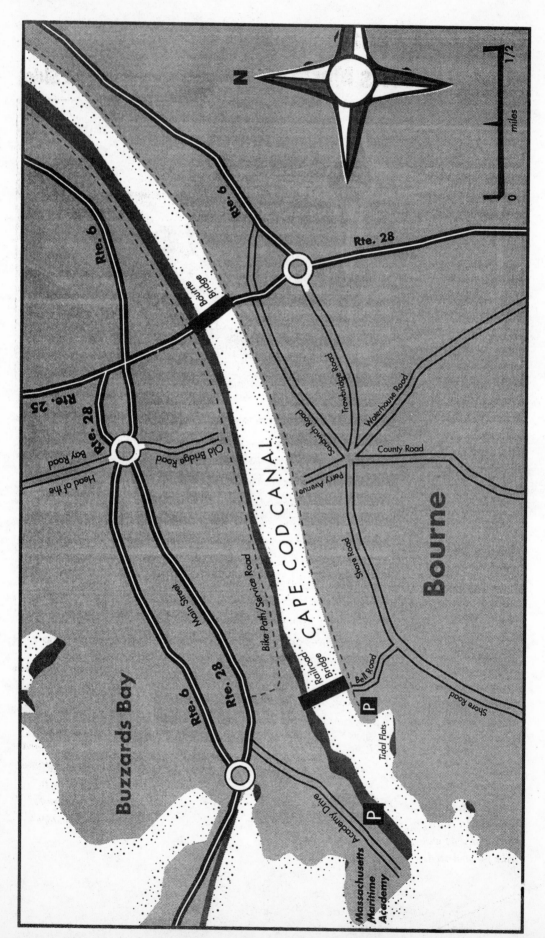

Cape Cod Canal
Massachusetts Maritime Academy (Mainland Side)

Parking spaces line this stretch of the Canal to the east of the MMA training ship.

In the years soon after World War II anglers such as Stan Gibbs and Stan Kuzia developed many fishing techniques and equipment for the Cape Cod Canal that are still used today. Plug fishing with wooden lures to imitate herring and menhaden and using leadhead jigs to get deep and defeat the swift Canal currents are two of their innovations. The early efforts by these and other anglers resulted in many of the lures that we take for granted.

An area of easy access with great fishing potential is the entrance of the **Massachusetts Maritime Academy**. Fishermen who throw plugs like this spot at first light, and the retaining wall to the east of the parking area is one of the few areas in the Canal where fishing an eel during the daylight hours can be very effective. No fishing is allowed off the docks of the academy.

In August and September bonito and false albacore are sometimes caught in this westerly end of the Canal. Some fishermen will take along two rods when fishing this area, one spinning or conventional rod for fishing heavy lures or bait and a lighter outfit set up with small lures or jigs in case these smaller members of the tuna family come charging through. During the brief periods of slack tide, it's also possible to catch scup, fluke and tautog around the riprap and in the deeper water near the docks.

Directions:
Off Main Street (Route 6) in Buzzards Bay, follow Academy Drive to the school entrance and parking area. Parking rules vary depending on MMA events.

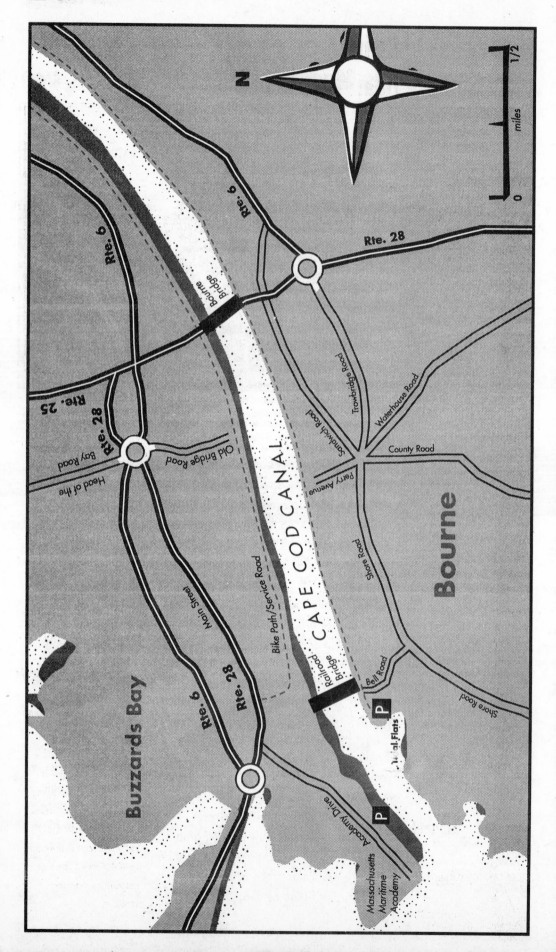

Cape Cod Canal, Railroad Bridge
Tidal Flats (Cape side)

Looking west, across the flats and the Canal, Massachusetts Maritime Academy is visible from the Bell Road parking area.

Many Canal fishermen customize their bicycles and cruise the paved access roads following the tide and searching for breaking fish. The access roads on both sides are elevated and run the length of the Canal, giving the biker a great view of the water. Many will wire a milk crate over the rear wheel to carry their tackle and attach rod holders to the sides of the crate.

The Tidal Flats are one of the most popular and productive locations along the Canal. Popular because the access is easy, there is plenty of parking and rest rooms are available, and productive because the lagoon at the end of the parking area is a veritable bait factory and opens directly into the Canal. Plug fishermen gather here in the predawn hours whenever there will be a "breaking tide," which is the brief time when the tide will be slack at dawn. This happens twice a month, and for a period of a few days striped bass are likely to be actively feeding on the surface. Some Canal fishermen prefer wooden topwater lures at these times.

In the spring try live-lining a herring off the point at the end of the parking area on a west tide. As the season progresses fishermen will use eels after dark for the hour or so that the current slows before low tide. Fly-fishermen wade out onto the flats in the lagoon and cast to schoolies that come into the shallow water after dark. First light can also be productive on these flats; just be careful not to venture too close to the edge of the Canal itself.

On the other end of the parking area is the Railroad Bridge, and stripers will hold on the downcurrent side of the bridge abutments waiting for baitfish to be swept past.

Directions:
From the rotary on the Cape side of the Bourne Bridge, follow Trowbridge Road to Shore Road, travelling southwest 1 1/4 miles to Bell Road on the right. Follow Bell Road to the Army Corps of Engineers parking area.

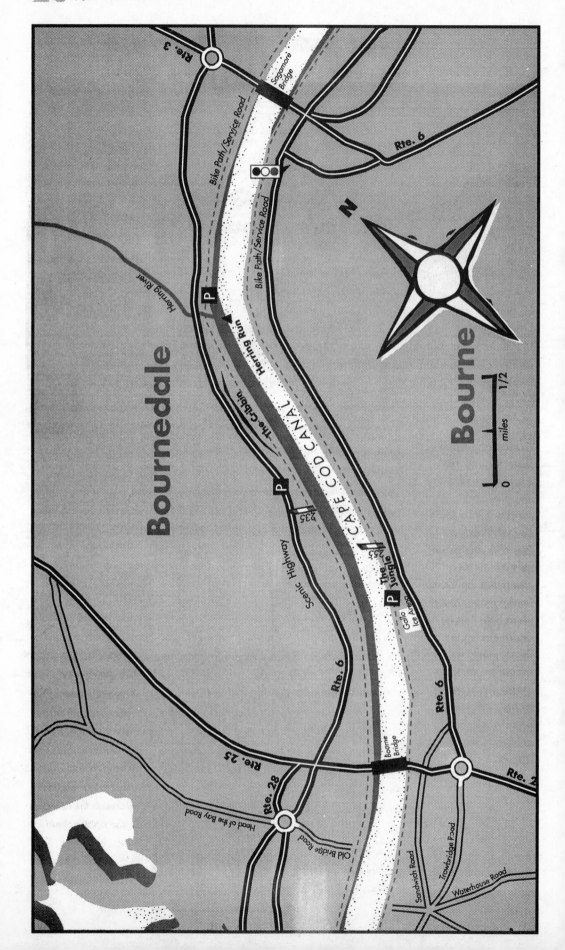

Cape Cod Canal, The Jungle
Pole 255 to Pole 265 (Cape side)

To the west of the Jungle is the Bourne Bridge.

Almost every fall fishermen in the Canal report seeing bluefin tuna, up to an estimated 100 pounds chasing bluefish. Occasionally one of the fishermen will even hook up with one of these fish. The result is always the same: a huge splash, a blinding run, an empty spool and a great fish story.

The Jungle and the Radar Tower are good alternatives to the Herring Run if that area is too crowded. Fish here on an east tide. From the Radar Tower, walk west to the next light pole. In front of the pole, start fishing one hour after the tide turns and stay for the next two hours. A nice rip sets up here, and this spot fishes well all season.

Directions:

From the rotary on the Cape Cod side of the Bourne Bridge, follow the Canal northeast on Sandwich Road for one mile to the Gallo Ice Arena on the left. Park to the right, behind the rink.

Cape Cod Canal, The Cribbin to The 100 Steps, Pole 220 to Pole 245 (mainland side)

The Cribbin got its name from the the cribbing, or retaining wall, that runs along what is known as the High Bank.

Eelskin plugs are still used on the Cape by some of the more traditional Canal and surf fishermen. A dried and salted eel skin is stretched over a swimming plug, such as a Danny or an Atom Swimmer, its tail left dangling behind the lure, or tied onto a specially designed leadhead with wired-on hooks. Fished very slowly around rocks or retrieved slowly across a rip, these lures can be deadly for large striped bass.

Named for an area of retaining walls along the north side of the Canal and a long set of steps that lead down to the area, **the Cribbin** location is best approached by bicycle down the access road. More than one angler has parked in the overlook area above, caught a nice bass and then wondered how he was going to drag the fish back up the 100 plus steps to his vehicle. This is a well-known early season tautog spot, along with being a great bass fishing area. On a west tide one to two hours after the turn, a good rip forms close to shore here. Try below pole 235, at the base of the steps where there is a mussel bed. Toward the end of a dropping west tide, move down to pole 245. This is a great spot to drift an eel after dark.

Directions:
From the Buzzards Bay Rotary travel 1.5 miles east on the Scenic Highway. The path to the 100 Steps is to the right of the Army Corps of Engineers sign. The path and stairs can be treacherous at night or in the predawn hours. Or continue another 1.1 miles to the Herring Run and bicycle west to the Cribbin.

Cape Cod Canal, The Herring Run, Bournedale (mainland side)

In May the riprap to either side of the Herring Run is a favorite with live-liners.

In spite of the popularity of modern spinning reels, many hardcore Cape fishermen prefer conventional or revolving spool reels for casting. In the hands of an experienced caster, these reels cast farther and more accurately than their spinning cousins and are less susceptible to line twist. The newer versions of these conventional reels have magnets or bushings to slow the spool down, making them less likely to back spin and snarl than the older models. They still require an "educated thumb," though, to slow the spool down as the lure reaches the water.

Around April 1, give or take a few days, the first scout herring will show up at the most famous fishing location on the Cape Cod Canal, **the Herring Run**. Fishermen will watch the run for some time before, waiting for this first sign that the season has started for another year. In the next few weeks more and more of these anadromous fish will return to their home stream, and the striped bass will follow. The Run has become so popular that the Town of Bourne requires anglers to purchase a license at the town hall, which allows them a few herring for bait, caught by a herring warden at the run.

Anglers then spread out near the run and live-line the herring or drift fresh dead ones in the Canal. Experienced anglers know that it's mandatory to fish the down-tide side of the run, particularly in the day during the last two hours of the incoming tide, right up to when the current slacks. At this time the warmest water, flowing in from Buzzards Bay, will bring in the majority of the stripers. The bite can continue for another two hours after the turn of the tide until the colder waters of Cape Cod Bay shut the fishing down. From mid-May into the first part of June, it's certain that large striped bass will be nearby, and many will be caught at the Herring Run.

Directions:
From the Sagamore Rotary intersection of Routes 3 and 6 on the north (mainland) side of the Canal, go southwest 1 mile on Scenic Highway to the parking area.

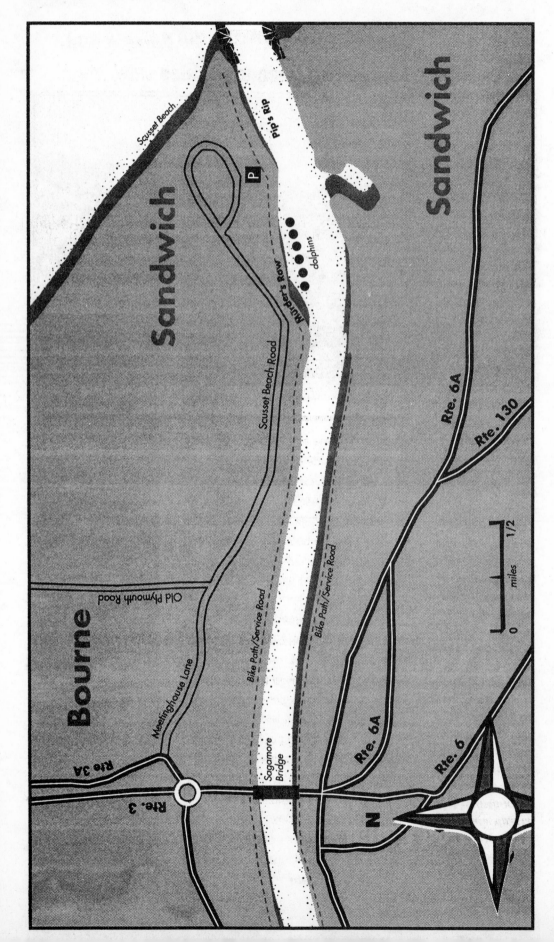

Cape Cod Canal, Pip's Rip to Murderer's Row, (mainland side)

Although shipping traffic has diminished in the Canal over the years, the pilings where large ships once tied up are still visible at the east end.

Hardcore bass fishermen know that a very slow retrieve of the lure or bait is often crucial for catching large stripers. The only exception to this general rule is in the Cape Cod Canal where fishermen using jigs will allow the lure to settle near the bottom, then use an aggressive upward motion with the rod tip to move the jig rapidly, bouncing it along the bottom. Reeling extremely quickly when nearing the riprap will minimize hang-ups.

Just south of the eastern end of the access road along the Canal, on the mainland side of the Canal, is an area known as **Pip's Rip**. The rock and mussel bed that extends out into the Canal is one of the few places that a fisherman can wade out, away from the rock riprap of the Canal banks, making this area a favorite of fly-fishermen who need room for a backcast. Bait fishermen also like this location because it's close to the eastern end of the Canal and features a sand bottom that is less likely to snag bottom rigs, a problem in other parts of the Big Ditch.

Because the water on the Cape Cod Bay side is much cooler than in Buzzard's Bay, the bite here can shut down or turn on very quickly with a turn of the tide. In the early season most fishermen prefer an east tide, which brings a surge of warmer water and tends to make the fish more active. About a half-mile west of Pip's Rip is an area called **Murderer's Row**, a favorite nighttime spot for fishermen who like to fish with eels. It's common to see fish feeding close to shore anywhere along this stretch, and because sand eels are often swept in from the Bay, a plug and teaser rig can be very productive here.

Directions:
From the Sagamore Bridge rotary at the end of Route 3, follow Scusset Beach Road east for 2 miles to the parking area at Scusset Beach State Reservation.

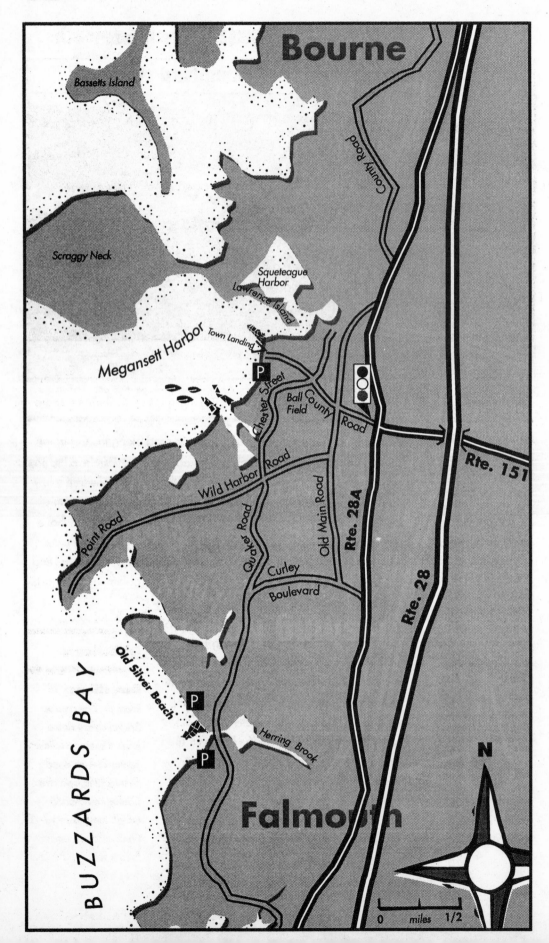

Old Silver Beach, North Falmouth

Herring Brook, the jetty and Old Silver Beach are visible from the parking area south of Herring Brook.

The two most common baitfish found close to shore around Cape Cod are silversides and sand eels. Silversides are more common on the Upper Cape where they spend most of their lives in the many estuaries and salt marshes and along beaches. Sand eels prefer the clear, tide-washed sand bottom of the Lower Cape. Both species are 2 to 6 inches long and occasionally longer. They are both thin bodied and best imitated with narrow-profiled lures or flies.

Old Silver is one of the better fishing spots on the western shore of the Cape. Unfortunately, it's also one of the better swimming beaches on the Upper Cape, so forget about fishing here during the day in the summer. The early morning, evening and after-dark fishing can be fabulous all season long though, so it's worth the effort.

An interesting feature of Old Silver is the stream and marsh that bisect the beach. This stream is a fairly good herring run, and in the spring natives-in-the-know drift live herring off the jetties. The outer beach area has plenty of sand eels and silversides, which makes it prime territory for the fly-rodder.

From July 4 through the end of August the Town of Falmouth chains off the entrances of the parking lots at night, making parking problematic. In the fall when the parking lots are open 24 hours a day, the fisherman will sometimes run into schools of baby herring leaving the stream between the beaches. If you're lucky enough to be there when this happens, you'll find stripers by the dozens waiting just off the beach.

Directions:
From Route 28 take the Route 151 exit. Go west for 1/4 mile on Route 151 to Route 28A. Proceed south on Route 28A for 1 mile. Then take a right onto Curley Boulevard, which merges into Quaker Road, and follow for 1 1/2 miles.

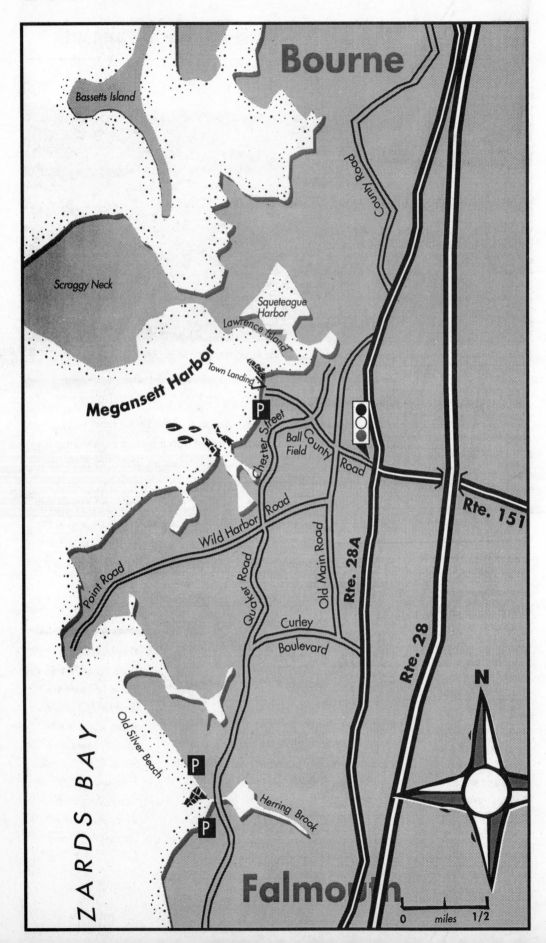

Megansett Harbor, Bourne/North Falmouth

The northwesterly view from the jetty at Megansett Harbor includes Scraggy Neck to the left and Lawrence Island to the right.

Modern soft baits such as grub tails, plastic worms and eels, shad bodies and artificial squid strips are very effective lures for striped bass. Taking a page from the freshwater fisherman's book, these artificials can be rigged weedless style and fished in places where traditional saltwater lures would hang up. An added advantage is that a single hook is used with most of these lures, which makes release of short fish much easier on both the fish and the fisherman.

In years past **Megansett Harbor** and its upper reaches, known as Squeteague Harbor, where known as a great place to look for large bluefish, particularly in the fall when huge schools of menhaden appeared. Fishermen soaking bait chunks or live-lining these oily baitfish would connect with blues up to 20 pounds. Unfortunately, as the schools of mature menhaden have become scarce in recent years, the bluefish catches have become less frequent, and the fish have been smaller.

The striped bass has made up for the lack of bluefish, and shore fishermen have even been connecting with fluke. Megansett Jetty is one of the few places where the shore-bound angler has a chance at bonito and false albacore, which show up in July and August.

Megansett has a pretty and lightly used town beach area, making it a great spot for an early evening family picnic combined with some good fishing!

Directions:

From Route 28 take the Route 151 exit. Go west 1/2 mile to Route 28A. Go straight through the lights onto County Road. Follow County Road through the center of North Falmouth, past the ball field, uphill and straight through the intersection. Continue to the harbor, parking on the left in the town parking lot.

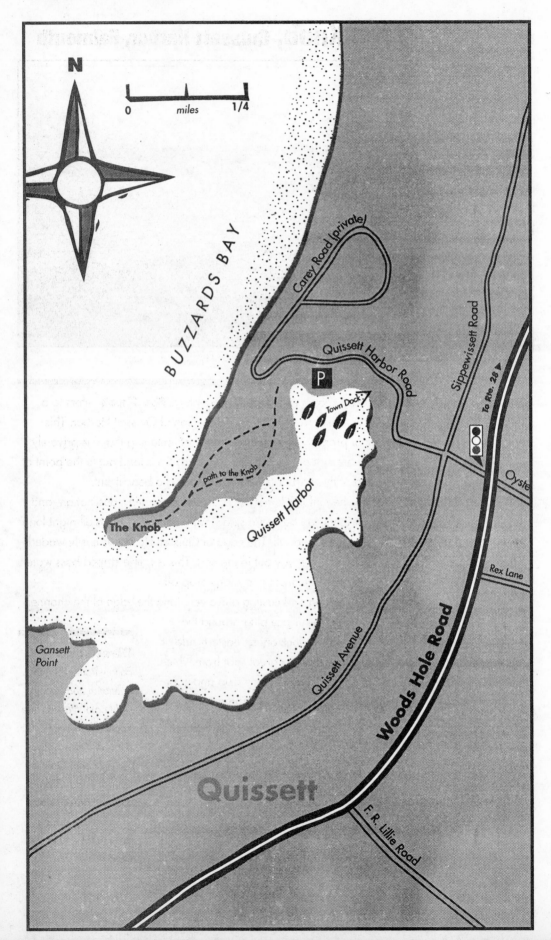

N

0   miles   1/4

BUZZARDS BAY

Carey Road (private)

Quissett Harbor Road

Sippewissett Road

To Rte. 28 ►

P

Town Dock

Oyste

path to the Knob

Quissett Harbor

Rex Lane

The Knob

Gansett
Point

Quissett Avenue

Woods Hole Road

Quissett

F. R. Lillie Road

The Knob, Quissett Harbor, Falmouth

The Knob is clearly visible to the southwest from the beach on Buzzards Bay.

An onshore wind may be hard to cast against, but it's usually more productive than an offshore breeze or flat calm conditions. Wind in your face pushes warm surface water and bait up against the shore and with it predatory striped bass and bluefish. Unfortunately, a few days of stiff onshore wind also pushes weed into the shallow water. In spite of these tough conditions, experienced surfcasters know that this is the best time to find a trophy fish.

The area known to Falmouth residents as **the Knob** refers to a large wooded tract on the northwest side of Quissett Harbor. This piece of property is a conservation trust, meaning that it is privately owned but that public access is allowed. Trails lead out to the point at the end of the Harbor (the Knob itself) and a beachfront.

This beautiful little harbor is a popular boating destination, and small stripers can be heard splashing among the yachts all night long in the summer and fall. The edge of Quissett Harbor is easily waded and fished all the way out to the end. This is prime striped bass water, with boulders, eelgrass and sharp drop-offs.

Try walking and casting a live eel along the edge of the channel or swimming a surface plug around the rocks. The town dock on the eastern side of the inner Harbor is a great spot from which children can bottom fish for scup and the occasional tautog or fluke. The outer beach is preferred by fly-fishermen who fish at night for large stripers.

Directions:
Follow Route 28 into Falmouth and bear right onto Woods Hole Road. Continue 1 1/2 miles and turn right at the light onto Quissett Harbor Road. Follow Quissett Harbor Road to the small parking area at the end of the road.

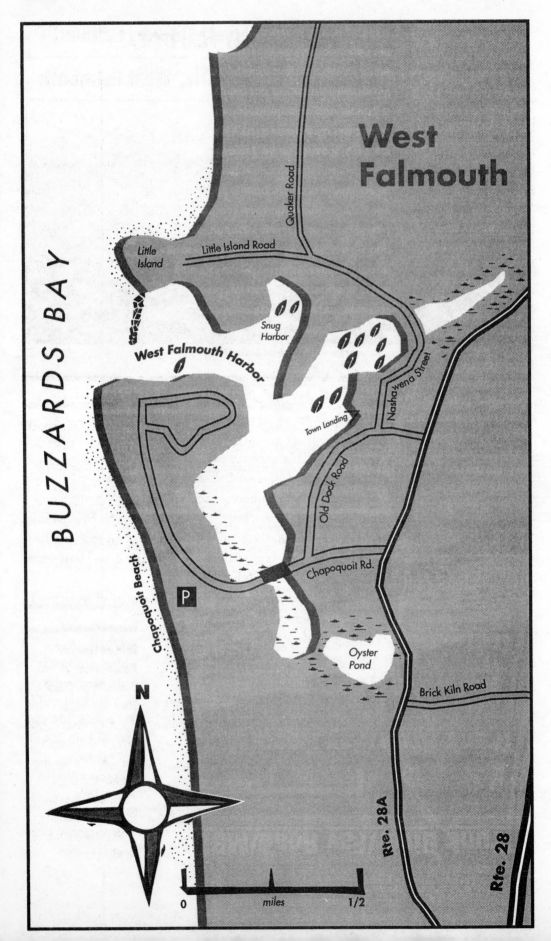

West Falmouth Harbor/ Chapoquoit Beach, West Falmouth

The town section of Chapoquoit Beach stretches from in front of the parking area to the south.

Salt water is a corrosive environment for all fishing tackle, and reels are particularly susceptible. Rinsing with fresh water will remove salt from the exterior of the reel, and a light coat of spray lubricant will help keep the salt off. With spinning reels, a periodic checking and cleaning of the drag washers will keep a reel performing like new. Take the spool off the reel and carefully remove the retaining spring over the washers. Invert the washers onto a pencil or screwdriver and wipe each one off with a clean, damp

This fishing area needs to be divided into two zones, the outer beach area at **Chapoquoit** and **West Falmouth Harbor**. The beachfront is a popular residents-only beach that is guarded from 8 A.M. until 5 P.M. in the summer. At these times the beach is so crowded with swimmers that a fisherman would have very little interest in wetting a line here anyway.

Predawn and in the evenings until well after dark, though, the fishing can be very productive. Silversides and sand eels are the predominant baitfish, and stripers can sometimes be heard and seen chasing these baits right up to the edge of the beach. Flies and small surface lures produce here all summer long, and fishermen who prefer fishing chunk baits, such as cut pogies and mackerel, sometimes catch very large bluefish, particularly on the north end of the beach near the rocks. The town beach extends for only a few hundred yards in front of the parking area. Even though the fisherman is within his rights to fish beyond the town beach, he must stay in the wet sand (inter-tidal) zone and must not cross higher onto the beach, which is private property.

Directions:
Take Route 28 south and exit at Brick Kiln Road. Head west on Brick Kiln Road for 1/4 mile to Route 28A. Go north on Route 28A for 1/2 mile to Chapoquoit Road on the left. Take Chapoquoit Road to the town parking lot at the public beach.

→   →

West Falmouth Harbor
Chapoquoit Beach, Continued

Chapoquoit Road bridges a section of inner West Falmouth Harbor and continues to the west.

cloth. Any fiber washers that are dry, brittle and impregnated with salt should be replaced. Be sure to place the washers back in the spool in the exact order in which they were removed, and that the metal washers with beveled edges fit into the housing correctly. And never, ever, put grease or lubricant on the washers. Although your drag will work smoothly for a short time, the fiber washers will soon flatten and the drag will not function.

Behind the beach, across the street from the parking area, are sand dunes, a shallow inlet and a grassy marsh that borders the inner harbor. Directly behind the dunes and along the marsh are clam flats where you'll find cruising stripers. Small swimming lures do the trick here, and the fly-fisherman will love this spot because it is one of the few places that a right-handed caster can put the predominantly southwest wind over his left shoulder and use it to his advantage.

To the south and east is the Chapoquoit Bridge, which crosses a shallow arm of the harbor. This is a great place to look for the worm spawns in May and early June that send the stripers into a frenzy. Don't expect to wade inside the bridge, as the bottom is soft, deep mud. Wading off the marsh to the north will take the angler along Chapoquoit Island. Remember that this exclusive community is strictly off limits above the high tide line.

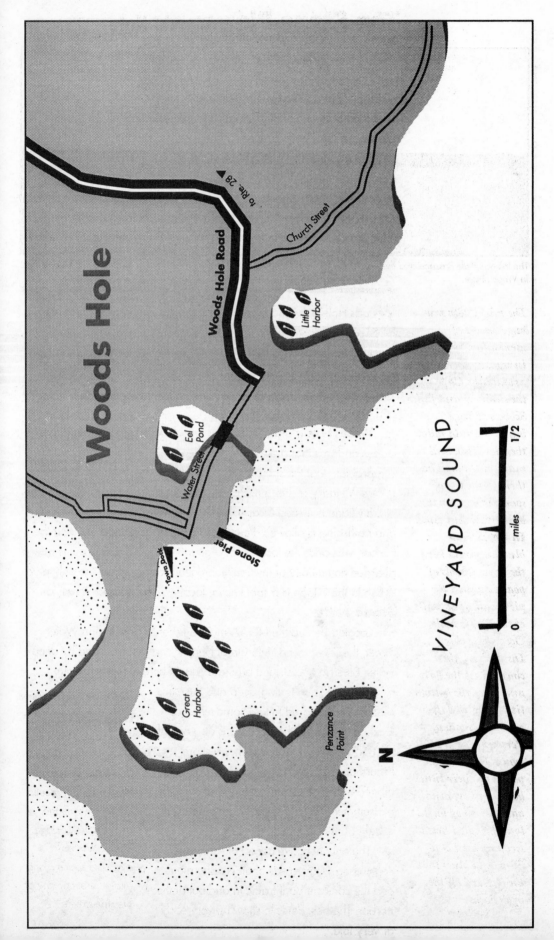

The Stone Pier, Woods Hole

The Woods Hole Passage and the start of the Elizabeth Island chain, Nonomesset Island, is visible from the Stone Pier in Woods Hole.

The mid-1980s saw huge schools of menhaden, or pogies, in most harbors around the Cape in the summer and fall. Schools of huge bluefish would follow these baitfish, and many fishermen had their first taste of sport fishing for these battlers at that time. In Woods Hole bluefish would herd the dense schools of pogies against the piers and stone walls of the Woods Hole Oceanographic Institution, then charge into the bait and leave the bottom littered with half-eaten menhaden. Personnel at WHOI would live-line the pogies on their lunch hour, and eventually had their shop build long-handled nets to scoop up the 12- to 20-pound blues that they hooked off the high docks.

Woods Hole is the most famous of the holes, or passages, between the Elizabeth Islands, which separate Buzzards Bay from Vineyard Sound. Although it's part of the town of Falmouth, the village is a distinct community. It is famous for its marine and oceanographic institutions and is the mainland port for the ferries to Martha's Vineyard and Nantucket.

Woods Hole is also well known for fabulous fishing around the ledges and rips that strike fear in the hearts of inexperienced boaters. The problem that the shore-bound angler encounters here is lack of access. Virtually all the shorefront is private property. Most of the shore in the village is owned or controlled by the various research institutions and no fishing is allowed. Penzance Point, the outermost point on the harbor, was once the location of a guano fertilizer factory, but is now a guarded community of multi-million-dollar homes. About the only place to fish in the village is a spot known locally as the **Stone Pier**, or **Stone Jetty**.

Located behind the NOAA marine fisheries building on Water Street, the jetty extends into Great Harbor and is surrounded by deep water. Bluefish and striped bass are caught here, and the bottom fisherman will find tautog, scup and fluke in season. Be prepared to lose some terminal tackle in the rocks, though. This is also one of the only places on the Cape that a shore fisherman has a shot at a bonito or false albacore when these southern fish show up in midsummer. A world-record bonito was caught off this jetty in 1998.

The only negative aspect of fishing here is contending with crowds of other fishermen and the constant boat traffic in and out of the harbor. The best bet is to show up very early or very late.

Directions:
Take Route 28 south toward Falmouth and follow the signs to Woods Hole. Proceed through the village, over the drawbridge, and park in any available space along Water Street or any of the side streets.

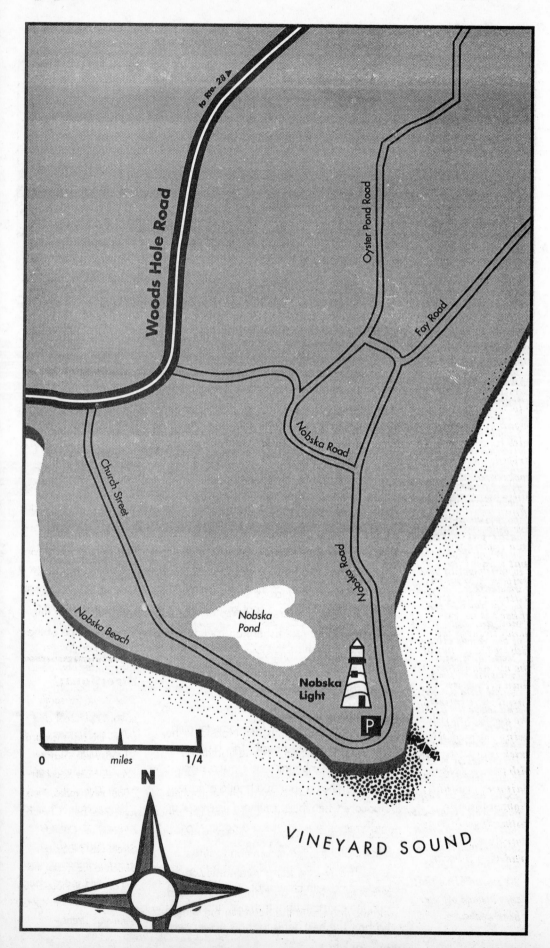

to Rte. 28 ▶

Woods Hole Road

Oyster Pond Road

Fay Road

Nobska Road

Church Street

Nobska Road

Nobska Pond

Nobska Beach

Nobska Light

P

0   miles   1/4

N

VINEYARD SOUND

Nobska Light, Falmouth

Look to the south from the beach at Nobska to see Nobska Light.

Circle hooks, sizes 6/0 to 9/0, are very popular for fishing with live eels for striped bass. These hooks were originally designed for tuna fishing and are now available in a lighter wire that is ideal for stripers. The main feature of this style of hook is its tendency to catch the fish in the corner of the mouth, rather than deep down inside, minimizing the damage to fish being released. The trick is to allow the fish to run with the bait and gradually tighten the line, rather than hitting sharply as with traditional hooks.

The rip that sets up in front of **Nobska Lighthouse** is, without a doubt, the most popular, productive and difficult fishing on the Upper Cape for the angler looking for a big bluefish or striped bass. What makes this spot so productive is the huge rip that runs on both an easterly (flood) tide and the preferred westerly (ebb) tide. And what makes it so difficult is the huge boulder field where most big fish are likely to run after being hooked.

To the left (east) side of the hill are the remains of a small jetty that's a preferred fishing location. Unfortunately, there's only room for one angler on its slippery rocks, forcing most fishermen to cast large popping plugs and surface swimmers between the large rocks around the point. Huge stripers are taken here on live eels drifted out on the tide and off the more fisherman-friendly beaches on either side of the bluff, usually in the late season or after dark.

Fly-fishermen also do very well off these adjacent beaches fishing small sand eel patterns.

The real bonus of fishing Nobska is the beautiful location, a bluff and lighthouse overlooking the Sound and Martha's Vineyard. This is one of the most photographed and painted spots on the Cape and a perfect place for a family picnic or an early morning photo shoot. It's not uncommon to find couples having wedding ceremonies on the bluff in the summer, and whales have been seen moving down the Sound in the winter and early spring.

Directions:
Take Route 28 south toward Falmouth and follow the signs toward Woods Hole. Stay on Woods Hole Road for about three miles, then take a left onto Church Street. Take Church Street past Nobska Beach to the top of the hill at the lighthouse.

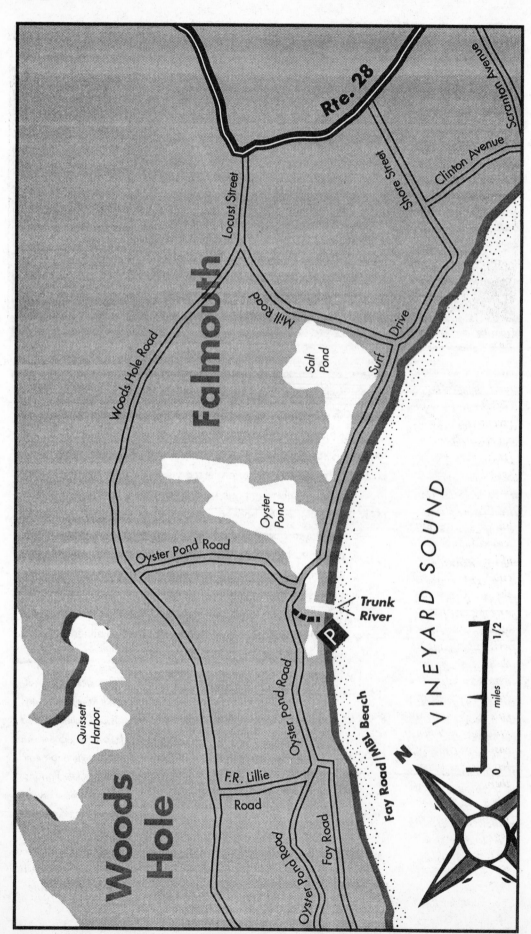

Rte. 28

Scranton Avenue

Clinton Avenue

Shore Street

Locust Street

Falmouth

Mill Road

Surf Drive

Salt Pond

Woods Hole Road

Oyster Pond

Oyster Pond Road

Quissett Harbor

Woods Hole

Oyster Pond Road

F.R. Lillie Road

Oyster Pond Road

Fay Road

Fay Road/MBL Beach

Trunk River

P

VINEYARD SOUND

N

1/2

miles

0

Trunk River/Fay Road/MBL Beach, Falmouth

From the Trunk River an angler can look to the southwest along Fay Road/MBL Beach and see Nobska Light in the distance.

Eels have become the most popular live bait for stripers in recent years. To keep an eel from tying itself in knots around your line, icing the bait is the important first step. Fill a bucket with damp seaweed, put in a bag of ice (not loose cubes!), and dump in the eels. Don't put any water in the bucket because the eels will quickly use up the oxygen in the water and die. The ice will put the eels into a dormant state, making them much easier to handle and less likely to twist themselves into a ball when put on a hook. Be sure to cover the top of the bucket with an old towel to keep the eels from escaping before they go to sleep. The towel will also give you a way to grip the slimy devils!

The beach across the bike path from the parking area at **Trunk River** (more appropriately called Trunk Trickle!) is open to the public and is the premier spot to swim a live herring in the spring or soak bait chunks later in the season. This is one of the more popular herring runs in town, but regulations change on a year-to-year basis, so be sure to check with town hall before taking any herring.

The fly-fishing along this stretch of beach can be very productive in the early and late season. Just watch your backcast or you may find yourself connected to a biker or Rollerblader on the popular bike path directly behind you! The beach to the south and west is fishable all the way to Nobska Lighthouse. The first two jetties that you'll encounter are favorite spots for the locals when they bottom fish or cast for stripers and bluefish. This area is known locally as the **Fay Road/MBL (Marine Biological Laboratory) Beach** and is private above the high-water mark, but the wading fisherman has plenty of good water to explore for almost two miles along the beachfront.

Directions:
Take Route 28 south toward Falmouth, follow the signs toward Woods Hole. Stay on Locust Street (Woods Hole Road) for 1/2 mile and take a left onto Mill Road. Follow Mill Road to the end. Take a right onto Surf Drive, follow the shore for 1 mile and bear left onto Oyster Pond Road. Follow Oyster Pond Road for 1/4 mile to an unmarked road on the left. Follow this road to the town parking area.

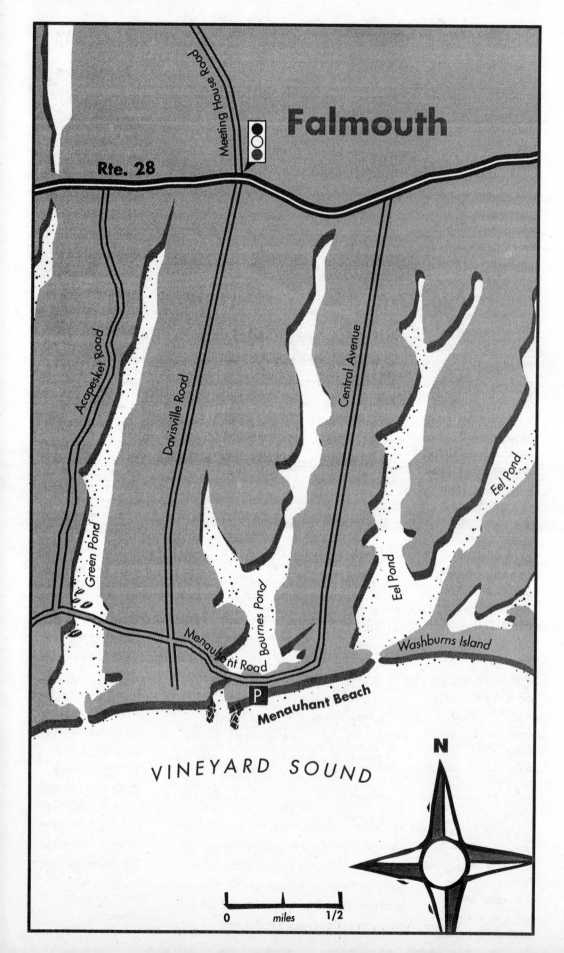

Meeting House Road

Falmouth

Rte. 28

Acapesket Road

Davisville Road

Central Avenue

Eel Pond

Green Pond

Eel Pond

Bournes Pond

Menauhant Road

Washburns Island

P

Menauhant Beach

VINEYARD SOUND

N

0   *miles*   1/2

Bournes Pond/Menauhant Beach, Falmouth

Bournes Pond fingers north (to the right) from the Menauhant Road bridge.

The cheapest insurance that a fisherman can buy is new line. Monofilament, dacron and nylon lines are strong and durable, but exposure to the elements will weaken them. With lure prices climbing higher all the time, many experienced fishermen avoid break-offs by replacing at least the last hundred yards or so a couple of times during the season. And stripping the spool at the end of the season allows the fisherman to see any corrosion on the interior of the spool.

Bournes Pond is one of a half-dozen salt ponds that line the south shore of Falmouth. Most of these ponds hold fish, but Bournes has, by far, the best access and parking. The outer beach area is a town-owned facility, which is popular with bathers.

In the evening it's common to find schoolies breaking along the edge of the beach, chasing silversides. Walk and cast along this beach to the east all the way to the entrance of Eel Pond, a section of Waquoit Bay. Bait dunkers will find this is an easy place to fish chunk herring, menhaden or mackerel for bluefish and stripers, or squid strips for fluke and scup, as the bottom is sand and gravel with very little on which to hang up your gear. The sandbar off the mouth of the pond changes on a yearly basis, but if the tide isn't running too hard, it's worth wading out and casting over the edge with small swimming plugs or soft baits, such as rubber shad tails.

The inside of the pond has become the most popular gathering place for local saltwater fly-fishermen and sometimes can get a little crowded. As the season progresses the stripers get quite sophisticated and the fly-rodder using sparsely tied sand eel and silverside imitations fished very slowly will score better than the person using large, flashy patterns. It's almost certain that a few local experts will be watching and will be happy to critique your efforts!

Directions:
Take Route 28 south into Falmouth. From Falmouth center go east and north on Route 28 for 5 miles. Take a right onto Davisville Road in East Falmouth. Follow Davisville Road for 1 1/2 miles to the stop sign. Take a left onto Menauhant Road and follow it for 1/2 mile to the town parking lots.

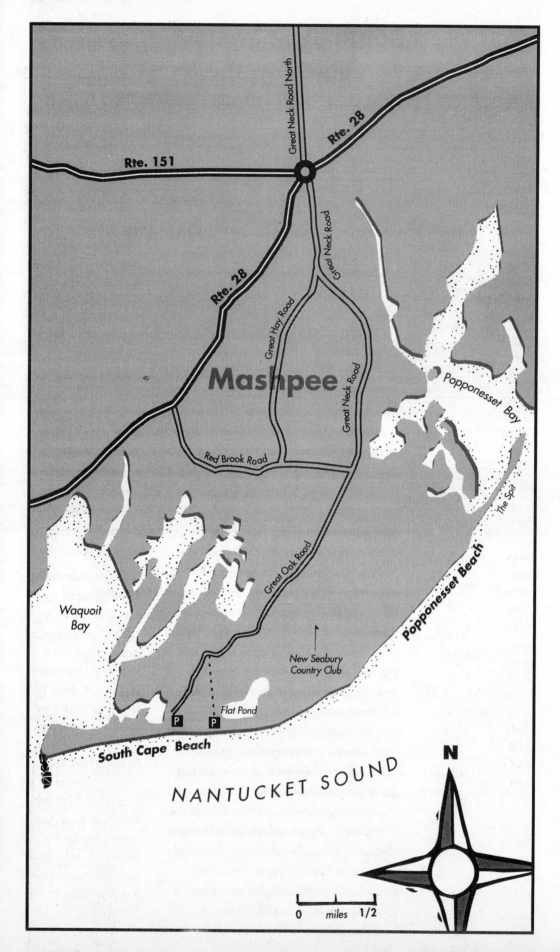

Rte. 151

Great Neck Road North

Rte. 28

Rte. 28

Great Neck Road

Great Hay Road

Great Neck Road

Mashpee

Popponesset Bay

Red Brook Road

The Spit

Great Oak Road

Popponesset Beach

Waquoit Bay

New Seabury Country Club

Flat Pond

South Cape Beach

NANTUCKET SOUND

N

0   miles   1/2

South Cape Beach/ Popponesset Beach, Mashpee

Anglers line the shore to the west of the parking area at South Cape Beach.

On Cape Cod one of the most popular and effective baits for all saltwater species, from scup to stripers, is the lowly seaworm. Most of the worms sold by bait shops on the Cape come from Maine, and can be expensive compared to other fresh baits. If the worms are not going to be used immediately, line the box with paper towels and refrigerate as soon as possible.

For reasons no one seems to understand, the first stripers and the first bluefish of the season seem to always show up somewhere along this six-mile beach. Around the middle of April striper fishermen start searching this shoreline, casting small metal lures, swimming plugs and flies, hoping to be the first to catch a newly arrived linesider. These first fish will be schoolies, with larger stripers arriving around the first week of May. Bluefish put in an appearance around the end of May, and it's not uncommon to see a dozen surfcasters with rods bent when the blues blitz in the evenings. Conventional and spin fishermen score best using surface plugs for these bluefish, and sometimes the action is so fast and furious that fishermen will remove the hooks from surface lures just to watch fish after fish bang their offering.

The beach directly in front of the parking lot is **South Cape**, which extends west for about 1 1/2 miles to a long jetty that marks

Directions:
Take Route 28 from Falmouth and follow it east and north for 8 miles to the intersection of Route 28, Route 151 and Great Neck Road at the Mashpee Rotary. Go south 2 1/2 miles on Great Neck Road to the intersection of Great Neck Road and Great Oak Road. Go straight through the intersection onto Great Oak Road, and follow it to South Cape Beach State Park.

→

South Cape Beach, Popponesset Beach, Mashpee

The Spit is at the end of Popponesset Beach, to the northeast.

the easterly entrance of Waquoit Bay. The bait fishing is good anywhere along this stretch with bluefish, fluke and scup being the primary targets. An ambitious angler can make the long walk to the Waquoit Bay entrance and find some great fishing, with after dark and early morning being the best times. A live eel drifted through the channel here can sometimes produce a memorable striper.

To the east, around the corner and in front of the New Seabury golf course, a small rip sets up close to the beach and is a favorite spot for the spin and fly-casting crowd. A weighted fly, such as a Clouser Minnow, cast out and allowed to tumble over the edge of the rip can often bring great results. From this point and for the next three miles of **Popponesset Beach** the bottom changes to gravel, small rocks and weed patches, prime striper water. The end of this beachfront is called the Spit and is a great spot, but unfortunately there's very little parking nearby. Check with local tackle shops for current access information.

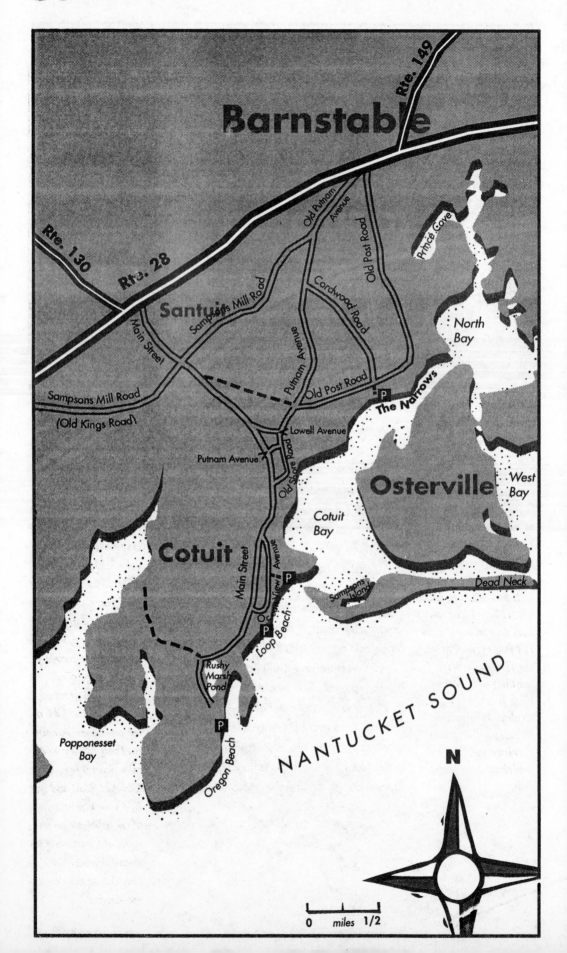

Rte. 149

Barnstable

Rte. 130

Rte. 28

Old Putnam Avenue

Old Post Road

Prince Cove

Santuit

Sampsons Mill Road

Cordwood Road

North Bay

Main Street

Putnam Avenue

Old Post Road

Sampsons Mill Road

(Old Kings Road)

Lowell Avenue

The Narrows

Putnam Avenue

Old Shore Road

Osterville

West Bay

Cotuit Bay

Cotuit

Main Street

Ocean View Avenue

Loop Beach

Sampsons Island

Dead Neck

Rushy Marsh Pond

Popponesset Bay

Oregon Beach

NANTUCKET SOUND

N

0   miles   1/2

The Narrows, Cotuit

The Narrows opens into North Bay to the northeast.

A very slow, steady retrieve is crucial when fishing live eels. It's also important to keep the rod tip high or off to the side. This will allow the angler to drop the rod or point it to the fish when the eel is picked up. Stripers will hardly ever hit an eel hard, the way they would a lure, so it's important to let the fish swim with the bait before the hook is set. The slightest hesitation or resistance to the retrieve may signal a pickup by a large fish.

Walk along the shore to the northeast, around the corner, for about 1/4 mile and you've arrived at one of the premier early season striped bass spots on the Cape. **The Narrows** is the junction between Cotuit Bay and North Bay and features a steep drop-off, a good rip and water that warms quickly in the spring. Farther into North Bay is Prince Cove, a favorite location for holdover stripers in the winter and early spring.

Whether the fish that are caught in April or May at the Narrows are holdovers or fresh-run fish is always a subject for debate among the locals, but no one argues that the fisherman armed with flies, small swimming plugs, soft baits and small jigs will score early and often. Soft-bodied, shad-type lures, in blue and white, have become quite popular here around the middle of May when the herring are running. This is also a good place for the fly-fisherman to look for worm spawns around the end of May.

Directions:

Take Route 28 to Main Street in Santuit. Go southeast on Main Street 1 1/4 miles to Lowell Avenue, which is on the left at a cemetery. Go left onto Lowell Avenue and proceed for 100 yards. Take a left on Putnam Avenue and continue for 1/4 mile. Take a right onto Old Post Road and go 3/4 mile to the Town Way To Water on the right. The parking is for Barnstable residents only during the day in the summer.

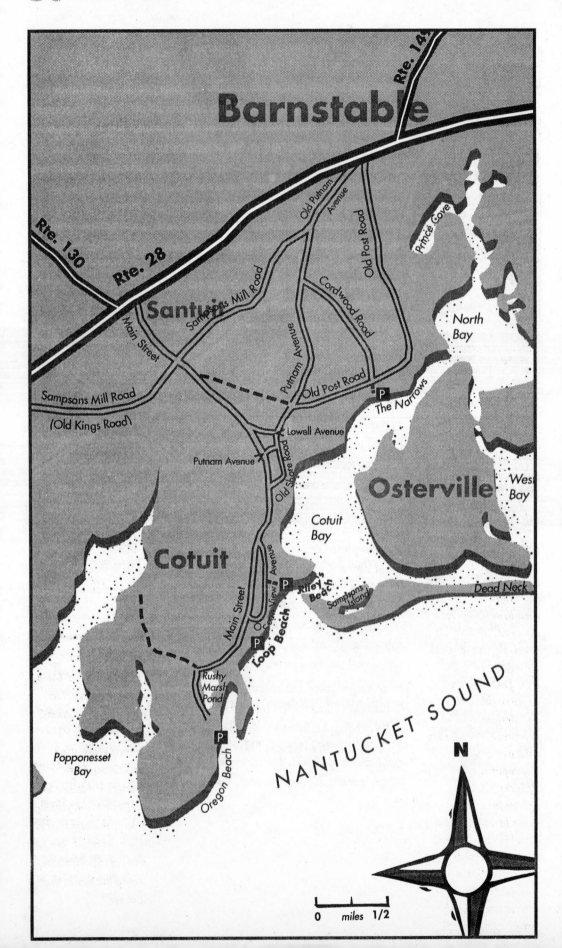

Barnstable

Rte. 14.

Rte. 130

Rte. 28

Santuit

Old Putnam Avenue

Cordwood Road

Old Post Road

Prince Cove

North Bay

Main Street

Sampsons Mill Road

Putnam Avenue

Old Post Road

The Narrows

West Bay

Sampsons Mill Road

(Old Kings Road)

Lowell Avenue

Putnam Avenue

Old Shore Road

Osterville

Cotuit Bay

Cotuit

Main Street

Ocean View Avenue

Riley's Beach

Sampsons Island

Dead Neck

Loop Beach

Rushy Marsh Pond

Popponesset Bay

Oregon Beach

NANTUCKET SOUND

N

0   miles 1/2

Loop Beach/Riley's Beach, Cotuit

From the southernmost parking area at Loop Beach, the entrance to Cotuit Bay can be seen in the distance.

Many fishermen fall into the habit of retrieving their lures at the same speed on every cast. Before changing lures, vary the speed at which the lure moves through the water. As a general rule, stripers like the lure to move slower, and bluefish prefer an erratic, fast retrieve. Some lures, such as needlefish and Danny-type surface swimmers, are designed to be retrieved very slowly and are more appropriate for stripers. Metal subsurface lures must be moved fairly quickly or they will snag the bottom, and their flashy, side-to-side motion is very attractive to bluefish.

The beach directly in front of the parking area is known as **Loop Beach**. As you proceed north toward Cotuit Bay, it becomes **Riley's**. These are private swimming beaches, but fishing is permitted anywhere below the high water line. Jetties and docks along the beach are private property.

This beach area has always been one of the first spots on the Cape to find bluefish, usually around the last week of May. Metal swimming lures are very popular, as are poppers. Local fly-rodders gather along Riley's Beach in the evenings, casting Clousers, Deceivers and sand eel patterns to the stripers that cruise the edge of the channel. They also appreciate the hill behind this beachfront, which offers some protection from the predominantly southwest and west wind.

In years when menhaden fill the inner harbor, chunk bait fished on the bottom in the narrow channel between Loop Beach and Sampsons Island produces large blues and stripers.

Directions:
Take Route 28 to Main Street in Santuit. Go south on Main Street 2 miles to Ocean View Avenue. Take a left onto Ocean View Avenue and follow for 1/2 mile to the parking area at the beach. This is a town beach that is open to residents only during the day in the summer.

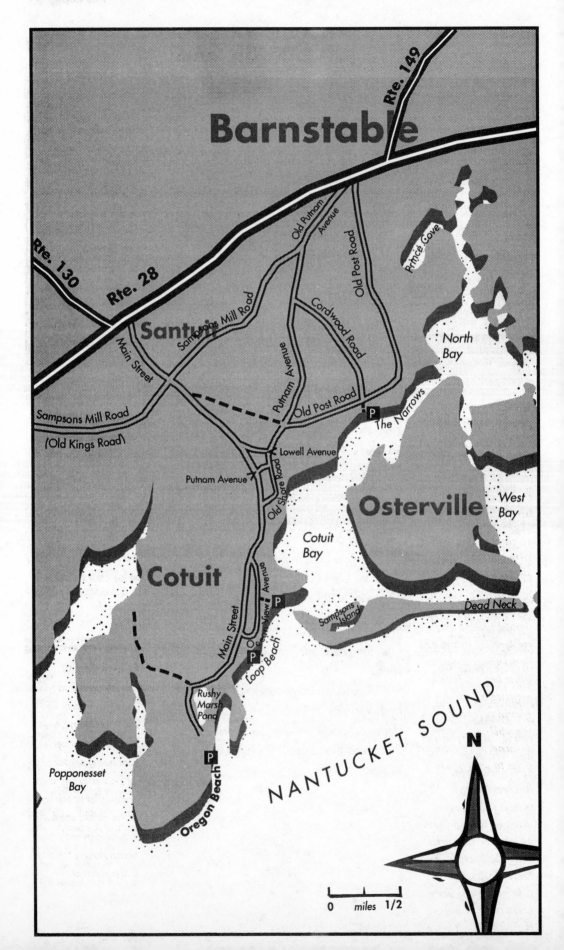

Rte. 149

Barnstable

Old Putnam Avenue

Old Post Road

Prince Cove

Rte. 130

Rte. 28

Sampsons Mill Road

Cordwood Road

Santui

North Bay

Main Street

Putnam Avenue

Old Post Road

Sampsons Mill Road

(Old Kings Road)

P

The Narrows

Lowell Avenue

Putnam Avenue

Old Shore Road

Osterville

West Bay

Cotuit Bay

Cotuit

Sampsons Island

Dead Neck

Main Street

Ocean View Avenue

P

P

Loop Beach

Rushy Marsh Pond

P

NANTUCKET SOUND

Popponesset Bay

Oregon Beach

N

0 miles 1/2

Oregon Beach, Cotuit

Oregon Beach faces Nantucket Sound.

Polarized sunglasses, a hat with a long brim and sun block are absolute essentials for anyone spending long days on the water. Many anglers prefer glasses with amber lenses, which will penetrate hazy sunshine and fog. A good hat should have a dark underside on the bill to minimize glare. Flats hats, which originated in Florida, feature a long bill and a brim around the back and sides to protect the neck.

Oregon Beach is another of the popular bluefish spots on the southern coast of the Cape. The shallow water off the shores of South Cape Beach, Popponesset and Cotuit warms quickly in the spring, and a strong southwest blow will bring out the local surfcasters looking for the early season blues.

The angler who is willing to walk a half-mile down the beach will eventually come to the eastern side of the entrance to Popponesset Bay, a prime bass and bluefish spot in the early morning and evening when the boat traffic subsides. Fluke and scup can be caught here also, with squid strips being the preferred bait.

Directions:

Take Route 28 to Main Street in Santuit. Go south on Main Street through Cotuit center, continuing a total of 3 1/2 miles to the town parking lot at the end of the public road. This is a resident-only town beach during the day in the summer.

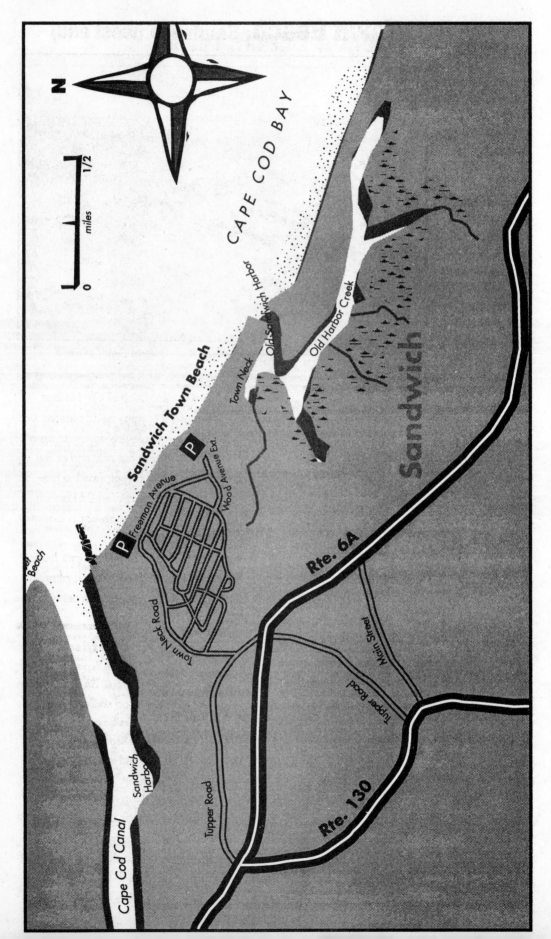

Town Beach, Sandwich (west end)

Looking northwest from the Freeman Avenue parking area, a barge can be seen exiting the Cape Cod Canal.

The Improved Clinch, Uni, Blood, Surgeon's, Surgeon's Loop, Albright and Nail are all basic knots that every fisherman should know. A poorly tied knot can reduce the breaking point of the line by more than half. Monofilament should always be moistened with saliva or water before a knot is pulled tightly.

Anglers heading farther east toward the entrance of Old Harbor often overlook **Town Beach**, but there are many good reasons to make this end of the beach a destination. Ample parking is adjacent to the beach, and it's a short walk to the jetty at the east end of the Canal. The jetty is a well-known and productive spot, and the preferred spots at the end of the jetty are usually occupied 24 hours a day at the height of the fishing season. (Non-slip footwear is essential on the weed-covered rocks at the water's edge.)

All the methods popular in the rest of the Canal can work here: plugging, drifting chunk or live bait and swimming live eels after dark. If the jetty is too crowded, the cove and beach area between the parking lot and the jetty is definitely worth a few casts. Because the Canal is so close, a good current runs along this beach and a live eel fished like a swimming plug late at night can yield great results. In the fall baby menhaden can be trapped in this cove for a week or more by marauding bass and blues, and when this happens, fly-rodders and light-tackle enthusiasts can have a field day.

Directions:
From Tupper Road (off Route 6A in Sandwich) go northeast 1 1/2 miles on Town Neck Road to the parking area.

Directly in front and to the east of the parking area is a long bar of cobblestone-sized and larger rocks that extends out into Cape Cod Bay. On a dropping (west) tide, wading fishermen will walk out on this bar and cast off the edges and around the boulders. A northeast wind that pushes bait in against the bar and beach is ideal in this location, but that same wind may also push in rafts of weed from the bay, making the beachfront unfishable.

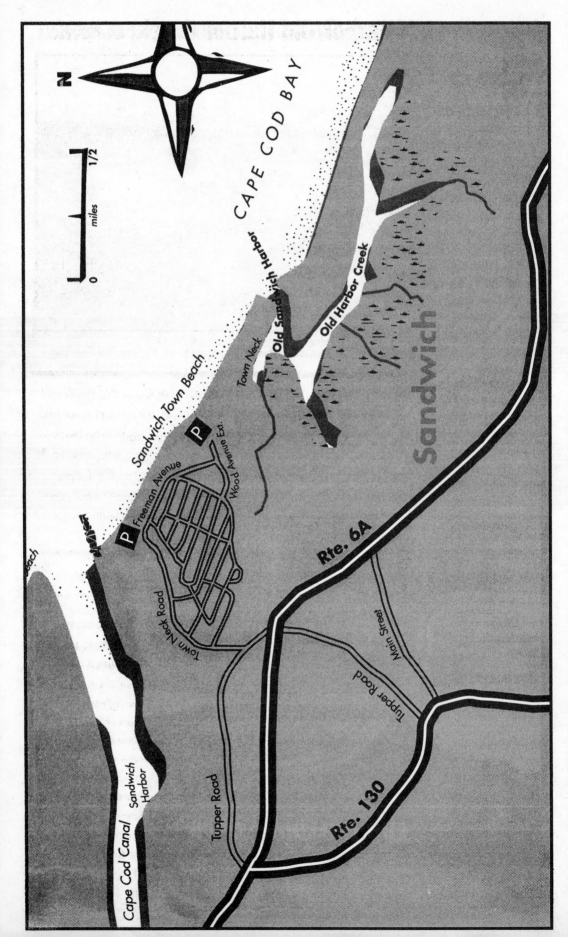

Old Sandwich Harbor/Old Harbor Creek, Sandwich

From Town Neck, Old Sandwich Harbor exits into Cape Cod Bay to the northeast.

For most saltwater fly-fishermen a stripping basket is as important a piece of equipment as their rod and reel. The basket is worn around the waist and may be homemade from a plastic dishpan or the store-bought type, which are curved and fit snugly against the body. All good baskets should have mono loops, plastic cones or some other protrusions on the inside to keep the fly line separated from itself while in the basket, minimizing tangles. Some anglers prefer baskets with holes in

→

One of the most picturesque spots on the upper Cape, the marsh and beachfront of what is known locally as **Old Harbor** is popular and productive. Fish anywhere along the public beach before the swimmers and beach-goers arrive or after they leave. This is a preferred spot for bait and bottom fishing because there is very little on the bottom that will hang up terminal tackle. Many fishermen feel that the big stripers and bluefish that move in and out of the east end of the Canal feed along this beach.

Walk to the east along the beach for 1/4 mile to find the entrance to the marsh. Two old jetties mark the entrance and the bottom changes from sand to cobblestone-sized rocks and gravel. This is great water for the fly- or plug fisherman. An evening high dropping tide is best at the height of the season, but fish can be caught here all day in the spring and fall.

Be extremely careful wading out on the bar off the end of the outlet. More than one fatality has occurred here, caused by the strong surge of water out of the marsh. This is particularly dangerous during extreme tides, which occur around the time of the full moon, new moon or storms. The marsh itself holds

→

Directions:
Off Route 6A in Sandwich, follow Tupper Road to Town Neck Road. Follow Town Neck Road for about 3/4 mile, and bear right onto Freeman Avenue. Follow Freeman Avenue to the end, and take a left onto Wood Avenue Extension. Follow this to the town beach. This is a fee parking area during the day in the summer; at all other times the lot is open free of charge.

Old Sandwich Harbor/Old Harbor Creek, Sandwich

Old Sandwich Harbor can be seen to the southeast of Town Neck when looking inland.

the bottom to allow water to drain out while fishing in high surf. Others prefer non-perforated designs; they feel that the line is less likely to be swept out of this type of basket by water that finds its way in.

fish all season long and fishes best after dark. But be sure to investigate the edges and bars in full daylight to locate likely feeding areas and dangerous footing.

The primary baitfish around Old Harbor are sand eels and silversides, although larger baitfish, such as menhaden, will sometimes find their way into the marsh. Brown trout, escapees from the state hatchery in Sandwich, are also occasionally caught in the upper reaches of the marsh.

Anglers should remember that a large marsh and estuary such as Old Harbor will take about an hour more to flood and ebb than the times given on tide charts for nearby areas. In other words, the tide may be fully high on the outer beach, but the water will continue to flow into the marsh with decreasing velocity for up to an hour. On the opposite end of the tide, water will flow out of the marsh for about an hour after listed low tides, and fishermen should plan their wading and fishing accordingly.

Old Harbor should not be confused with Sandwich Harbor, which is adjacent to the power plant off the Cape Cod Canal.

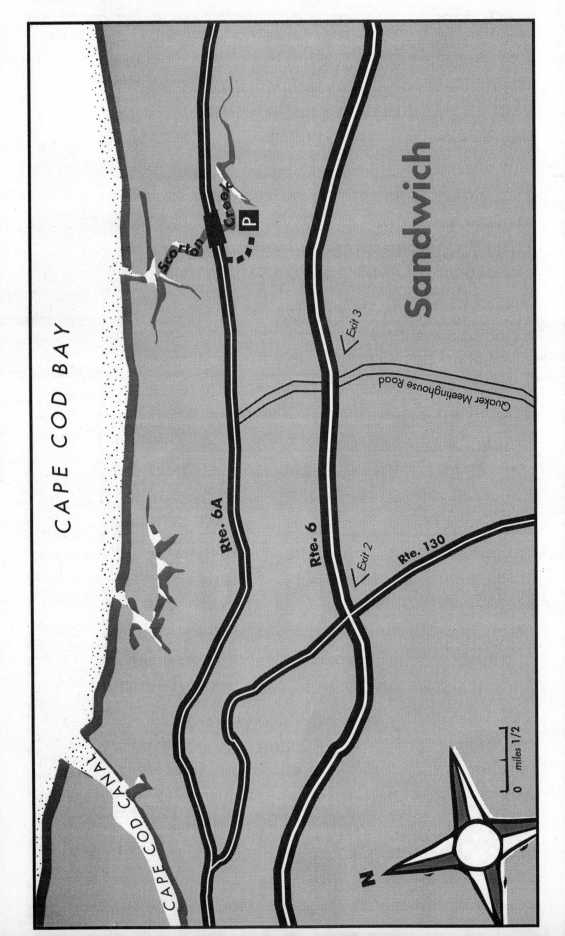

Scorton Creek (Upper), Sandwich

Scorton Creek empties into Cape Cod Bay to the north.

Scorton Creek in Sandwich is famous for sea-run brown trout and striped bass fishing year-round. For a few years in the 1970s, Scorton also held some Coho salmon, refugees from a failed stocking program in the North River in Marshfield. Although very few of these salmon were caught, quite a few were seen rolling in the pools above Route 6A. Occasionally, a lucky angler would hook into one of these fish, which weighed between 5 and 12 pounds, only to break off because →

The upper portion of **Scorton Creek** is not a shore location in the typical sense, but bears mentioning because it is a unique fishery on the Cape, offering year-round striped bass fishing and the possibility of hooking up with an elusive sea-run brown trout. There is plenty of forage for the fish throughout the length of the stream in the form of sand eels, mummichogs, silversides, small shrimp and crabs. Because the water inside stays warmer than the outside ocean in all but the coldest winter months, the stripers will stay and feed here all year. Many locals have stories of releasing dozens of fish on days in January and February when snow and ice cover the marsh.

Hickory shad cruise the upper reaches of the stream in the cold-weather months also, looking like schools of small bluefish as they ascend up stream from the ocean. The state stocks brown trout in Scorton, and the ones that are not caught immediately or disappear into the Bay quickly become acclimated and are extremely difficult to catch. The local line about these trout is that it takes "a thousand casts per fish."

There is debate about which stage of the tide is best in Scorton, but many anglers →

Directions:
From the junction of Routes 130 and 6A in Sandwich, go east on Route 6A for about 5 1/2 miles. Take the last right before the bridge over the creek. This dirt road follows the creek for 1/4 mile to a state-owned parking area.

Scorton Creek (Upper), Sandwich

Upper Scorton Creek stretches to the east from the parking area.

the tackle used was typically meant to handle 16- to 20-inch trout. Rumors persisted for years afterward that the fish were spawning in the river and had established themselves, but none were caught after the early 1980s.

prefer the dropping tide. One effective way to fish much of the upper portion is to launch a canoe, kayak or small aluminum boat two hours before high tide, fish up stream with the tide and then fish back down to the parking area as the tide drops. Be sure to plan any watercraft expeditions carefully, as it is almost impossible to paddle or row against the 6- to 8-foot tide.

It's also important to be very careful around the edges of the marsh and the drainage ditches that run through it. These edges can cover undercuts by the stream and can easily break off. The ditches are, in most cases, wider than they appear and feature bottomless mud. The wise angler walks far away from the stream before he or she tries to jump these ditches.

Light- to medium-weight spin or conventional tackle is sufficient here, as are small metal or swimming lures that will match the size of the baitfish. A fly-fisherman should use a high density sinking line, at least 325 grains and a weighted fly when the tide is running hard.

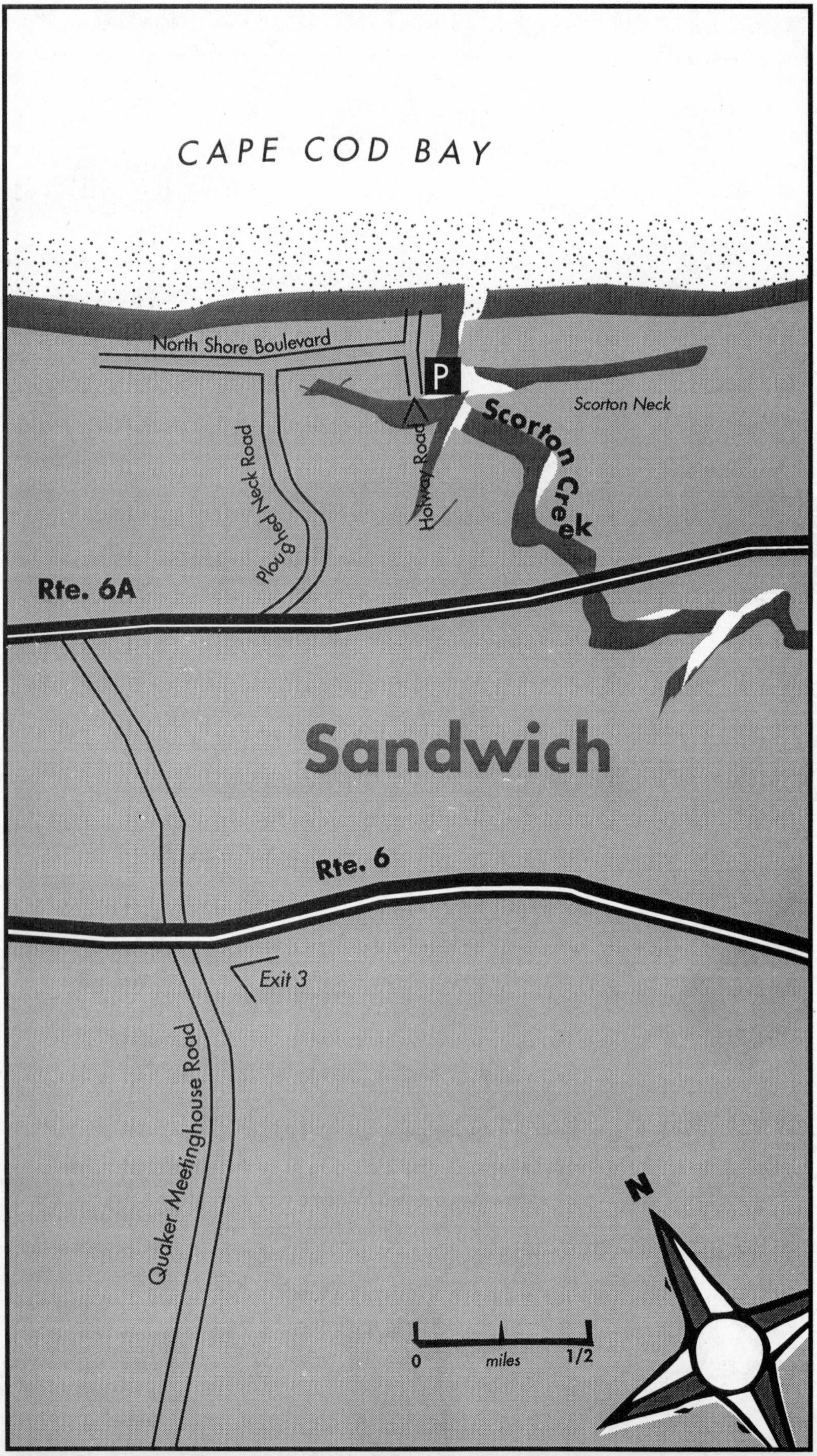

CAPE COD BAY

North Shore Boulevard

P

Scorton Neck

Scorton Creek

Ploughed Neck Road

Halway Road

Rte. 6A

Sandwich

Rte. 6

Exit 3

Quaker Meetinghouse Road

N

0   *miles*   1/2

Scorton Creek (Lower/mouth) Sandwich

Walking from the parking area around the corner to the north, an angler will see the converging waters at the mouth of Scorton Creek that fish favor.

When chasing schoolie bass, go light for more fun. A 7- to 8-foot rod rigged with 10- or 12-pound-test line is more than adequate to handle 16- to 20-inch stripers and even larger fish if the reel has a good, smooth drag. If fishing near rocks and jetties or if the bluefish are around, add a short section of heavier monofilament, 30- or 40-pound-test, between the lure and the running line for added insurance.

On an incoming tide stripers and occasionally bluefish will follow **Scorton Creek** into the marsh. If the tide is low and has just started to come in, the fish will be concentrated in the pools up stream to Route 6A. This can be a hazardous time to fish, however, because the water rises quickly and the mud banks on either side are very difficult to climb. Most fishermen head around the corner to the outer beach area, particularly as high tide just turns and is dropping. Many fish are caught in the deep channel that is formed at the narrowest part of the opening. Deep-running swimming plugs are used, or eels can be drifted here after dark.

At the mouth of the creek a gravel bar forms and can be waded at the lower stages of the tide. Extreme caution should be exercised here, also. Many anglers wear self-inflating personal floatation devices here after an unlucky fisherman was swept away and drowned.

Fast sinking fly lines are the rule for the fly-fisherman, and deep-running plugs in the channel have accounted for some very nice stripers and bluefish. Chunk bait fished on the bottom along the edges of the channel can also be effective. Scorton Creek and its mouth are great fishing spots at night, but should definitely be scouted out during the day.

Directions:
Off Route 6A in East Sandwich, follow Ploughed Neck Road north for 3/4 mile. Take a right onto North Shore Boulevard and follow to Holway Road Take a right onto Holway Road. There is parking for three or four cars straight ahead, or (with four-wheel drive) park on the sand area at the end of the road. Note the high tide line on the sand.

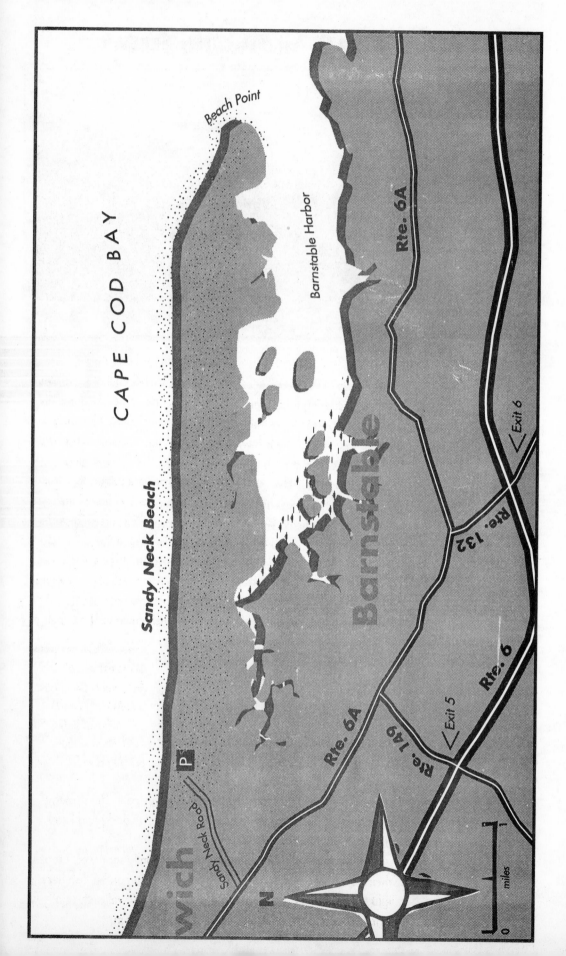

Sandy Neck Beach, Sandwich/Barnstable

Looking west along Sandy Neck Beach, the angler will find productive sandbars to his right in Cape Cod Bay.

Many anglers routinely carry one of the new multi-tools on their belt. Although these tools are expensive, most contain not only a knife blade and pliers, but also practical items like screwdrivers and files. Field repairs of equipment are often necessary and these lightweight, high quality tools can save the day. Be sure to rinse them off in fresh water after a day of fishing, however. Even though most are made of stainless steel, there are different grades of stainless and some are prone to corrosion after prolonged use.

Administered jointly by the towns of Sandwich and Barnstable, **Sandy Neck** is a beautiful, seven-mile barrier beach that separates Cape Cod Bay and Barnstable Harbor. This is one of the few areas on the upper Cape where vehicles are allowed on the beach. Camping is allowed in self-contained vehicles and families have been coming here for generations to enjoy the spectacular scenery and great fishing. Permits must be obtained at the gate and vehicles are subject to inspection for required safety devices and equipment. A four-wheel-drive vehicle allows access to some of the prime fishing areas, including the bars and rips at the end of the peninsula, Beach Point.

For the angler without motorized transportation, there are still good options. Although a guard occupies the gatehouse at the parking area 24 hours a day, fishermen are usually given free access after beach-goers leave and in the off season. Bait fishermen will time their efforts to coincide with the two-hour period on either side of high tide. Large bass and bluefish can be caught quite close to the beach at this time, particularly if it occurs at sunrise or sunset.

The most effective way to fish Sandy Neck, however, requires a fair amount of hiking and searching for fishy water. At certain places along the beach, weed patches are close to shore and provide cover for surprisingly large stripers. The strategy here is to travel light, use your eyes (and ears after dark) and keep casting as you work your way down the beach.

Fly-fishermen will appreciate the predominantly southwest breeze at their backs. Because sand eels are the most common baitfish here, a light-line spin or conventional angler can do very well with small jigs or thin-profile soft baits bounced along the bottom.

Directions:
From Route 6A in East Sandwich, go north 1 1/2 miles on Sandy Neck Road to the parking area.

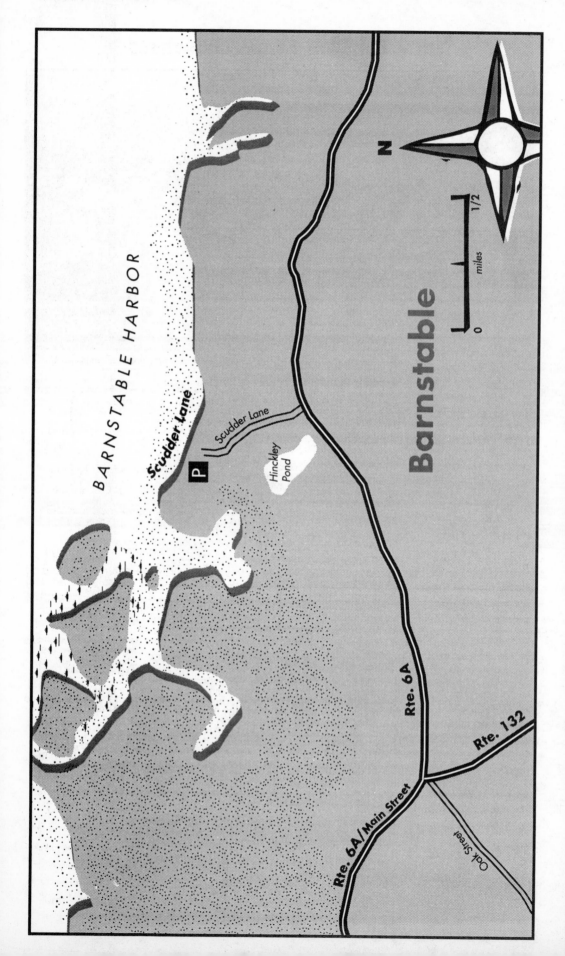

Scudder Lane, Barnstable

Rocky structure, a rarity on the Bay side of the Cape, can be seen looking in an easterly direction from the parking area at the end of Scudder Lane.

The typical outfit used by a Cape saltwater fly-fisherman is a 9-foot, 9-weight rod, a single-action reel with a disc drag and an intermediate, slow-sinking line. Most experienced fly-fishers also carry a spare spool loaded with a faster sinking line, weighing 250 to 350 grains, and another spool with floating line. The intermediate line is used most of the time, but the high-density sinking line could be needed in fast currents when the fish are feeding deep. The floating line allows the angler to fish surface flies, such as sliders and poppers.

The shoreline near the town parking area at **Scudder Lane** is one of the only parts of Barnstable Harbor that features rocks and underwater structure. The gradually sloping bottom can be waded easily near the ramp at low tide. The fish will be concentrated in a slightly deeper channel about 100 feet out. At high tide, particularly after dark or in the hour or so before dawn, fish will feed along the grassy end of the marsh to the east.

Walking to the west along the shore, the angler will find large boulders and the remains of old jetties. These are natural bait-holding areas, and stripers can be caught quite close to shore here.

About 1/4 mile west of the parking area the shoreline turns to the south. This point is a preferred fishing location. A nice rip sets up just off this point and the fish wait in the deeper water. This is a great place to drift an eel or swim a fly across the current. Occasionally, holdover stripers are caught in this part of the Harbor in the dead of winter.

Directions:

From the junction of Routes 132 and 6A, go east on Route 6A for 1 1/2 miles to Scudder Lane, which is on the left. Follow Scudder Lane to the ramp and town parking area. Parking is allowed here only with a town sticker during the summer.

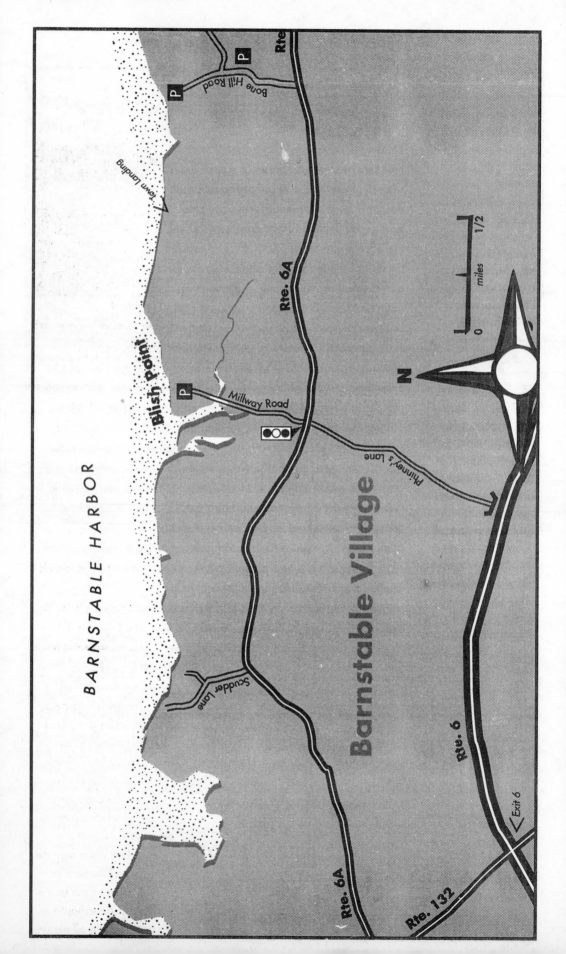

Blish Point, Barnstable

The town beach at Blish Point stretches to the east from the parking area at the end of Millway Road.

Waders have changed radically from the heavy rubber types of years ago. Modern waders may be made of canvas and rubber, treated nylon, neoprene or new, breathable, waterproof materials. The canvas and rubber types are the most abrasion resistant. In the summer months, the light-weight nylon and new breathable types are the most comfortable. Neoprene is flexible, has wonderful insulating qualities and is buoyant, in the event that the fisherman takes a spill.

The area around **Blish Point** has the best shore access on Barnstable Harbor and features a gradual sand bottom that's easily waded. The entrance to the inner harbor and channel to the west of the public beach are good spots to check out on a dropping tide as the water sweeps over the shallow bar on the east side. Consult the appropriate tide tables to coordinate wading with a dropping tide.

In the spring it's common to see hundreds of terns diving on sand eels, which are being driven to the surface by school after school of feeding stripers. In the late summer and fall menhaden invade the Harbor with bluefish and big stripers close behind. To the east of the public beach, a series of sandbars are revealed as the tide drops. Stripers cruise the troughs between the bars looking for bait, which is concentrated in the channels.

About 1/4 mile off the beach is one of the main channels, which drops to depths of ten to fifteen feet—even at low tide. Experienced local anglers will follow the dropping tide out to this edge, fish it for about a half-hour, then start fishing their way back to the beach. Resist the temptation to stay out on the sandbars as the tide floods, even if the fishing is good, which it frequently is. The tide rises and falls six inches every fifteen minutes in Barnstable Harbor, even faster on a flood tide combined with an east wind. It's very easy to find yourself on a rapidly disappearing sandbar with over-your-waders water on every side.

A small compass is an essential piece of equipment here too, as the fog can roll in faster than the fisherman can retreat to the beach.

Directions:

From the center of Barnstable Village on Route 6A, go north at the traffic light onto Millway Road. Follow Millway Road to the town beach parking area, which is only accessible with a parking sticker from the Town of Barnstable during the summer. It is accessible without a sticker in the off season.

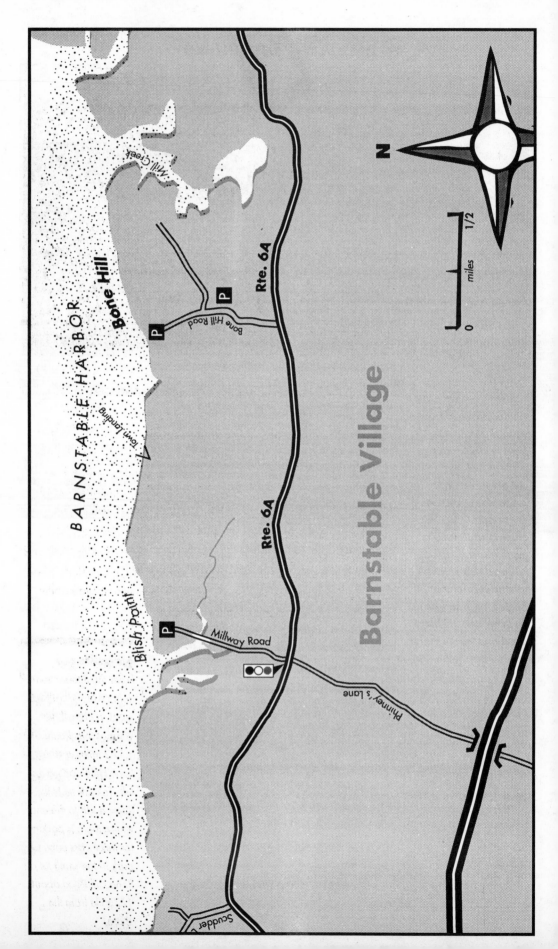

Bone Hill, Barnstable

The marsh edge at Bone Hill leads east toward the entrance of Mill Creek.

Whenever possible, tie directly to the lure or use a snap or snap swivel when striper fishing. Steel leaders are unnecessary and in fact may impair the lure's performance. Also, stripers see very well and a steel leader will spook wary fish feeding over a clear, sand bottom.

Bone Hill is the outer part of Barnstable Harbor, a popular location with anglers who like to wade and fish. Follow the dropping tide out from the parking area and fish the deep edges and channels between the bars. About 3/4 mile east of the parking area is the entrance to Mill Creek, a small estuary that empties into the Harbor. As the tide recedes it's possible to follow the channel of Mill Creek quite far out and catch stripers, which feed on abundant sand eels. As with the rest of Barnstable Harbor, it's crucial to watch the tide and start back in as the tide starts to flood. At high tide, particularly after dark, bass cruise along the marsh edge. Fishermen will walk softly along these edges, listening for the sound of stripers taking baitfish in the shallow water.

Directions:
From the intersection of Route 6A and Millway Road in Barnstable Village, take Route 6A 1 1/2 miles east to Bone Hill Road on the left. Take Bone Hill Road north to the end where there is parking for three cars only. Or park in the small lot on Bone Hill Road about 1/3 mile from the shore.

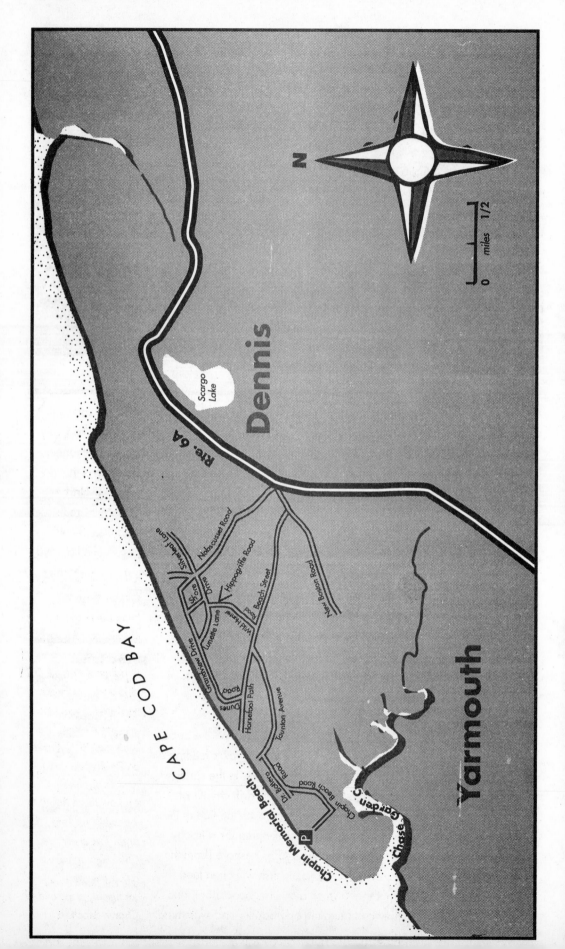

Chapin Memorial Beach/Chase Garden Creek,
Dennis/Yarmouth

The entrance of Chase Garden Creek can be seen to the southwest from Chapin Memorial Beach.

Sea birds diving on bait are a good sign of feeding stripers or bluefish. But the same birds congregating on shore-side rock piles or beaches are another good sign that bait and, possibly, predatory sportfish are nearby. Birds tend to stay where they've recently found a concentration of baitfish. Cormorants, a black, diving sea bird that's found all over Cape Cod, are a particularly good indicator that silversides, sand eels or other small fish are present.

The beaches on the Cape Cod Bay side of the Cape are generally lacking in structure, so it's important to seek out locations that are close to tidal rivers or estuaries, where there is tidal flow and cover for baitfish. **Chapin Beach** and **Chase Garden Creek**, the estuary on the south end of the beach, fit this requirement well.

Chapin is a popular bathing beach and, therefore, is best fished before dawn or after dark in the summer. On the north end of the beach is a community of summer cottages and motels. The lights from these buildings attract sand eels and other baitfish on warm summer evenings, and stripers can often be caught by fishermen wading out with a dropping tide.

Be sure to consult a tide chart before fishing here because, as with other areas of Cape Cod Bay, water depth can change quickly and dangerously as the tide rises.

The estuary and marsh behind the beach are good places to look for stripers feeding at night along the grassy banks. In the spring and fall bait fishermen will drift chunks of herring or menhaden out with the tide at the entrance of the marsh, hoping for a trophy fish. When the wind turns onshore (from the north or east), big bluefish will often feed right in the wash along the beachfront, and they can be taken on poppers and swimming plugs.

Directions:
From Route 6A in Dennis, go west for 0.2 mile on New Boston Road, northwest for 0.8 mile on Beach Street, west for 0.5 mile on Taunton Avenue, southwest for 0.7 mile on Dr. Bothelo Road (which becomes Chapin Beach Road) to the public parking area. The entrance to Chase Garden Creek is a 0.5-mile walk southwest, at the end of Chapin Beach.

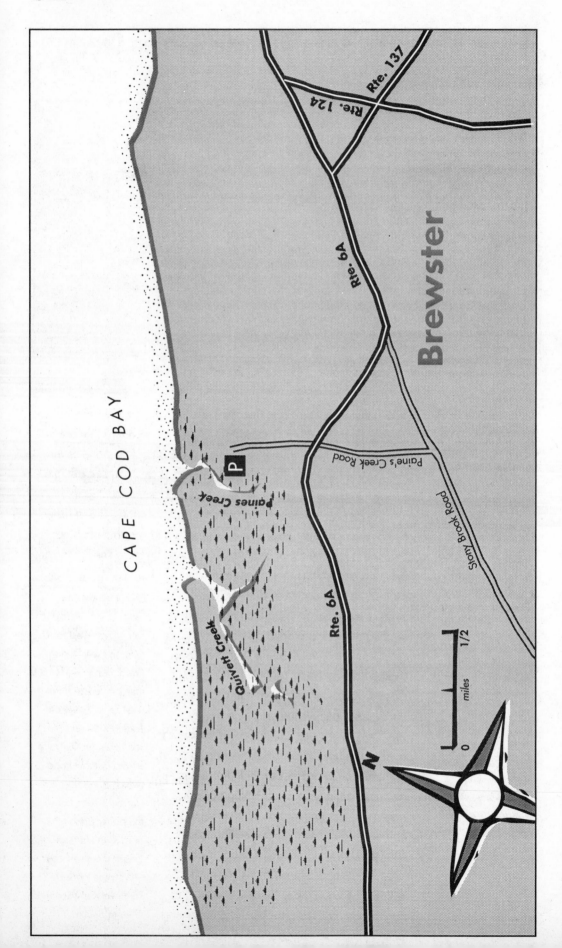

Paine's Creek/Quivett Creek, Brewster

Paine's Creek opens into Cape Cod Bay to the north.

Most anglers prefer a dropping tide when fishing the outlets of salt ponds, estuaries and harbors. Bait is swept out as the tide recedes; stripers and bluefish take advantage of this concentration of food. A lure, fly or live bait offering should be cast crosscurrent, allowed to swing out and retrieved at slow to moderate speed for stripers, faster for bluefish.

Paine's Creek and **Quivett Creek** in Brewster are both tidal estuaries that flow into Cape Cod Bay. The area off the beach is called Brewster Flats and is filled with stripers in the late spring. Wading fishermen should plan to fish on a dropping tide, preferably in the predawn hours and at first light in the morning. Many stripers are caught at the mouths of the creeks just after high tide. Paine's Creek is adjacent to the parking area and Quivett is 1/2 mile to the southwest. Both feature a channel that runs out from the beach, bordered by grass and sandflats. Fly-fishermen love this area where big stripers can often be seen chasing sand eels in shallow water. If no fish are showing, cast into the darker water over the grass patches. Because of the large rise and fall of the tides on the Bay side of the Cape, it's important to begin working back toward the beach as the tide floods.

Directions:

From the junction of Routes 6A and 137, go west for 1 1/4 miles on Route 6A to Paine's Creek Road on the right. Follow Paine's Creek Road for 1/2 mile to a parking area. A town sticker is required for parking here in the summer, but the area is accessible before June 1 and after Labor Day without a fee.

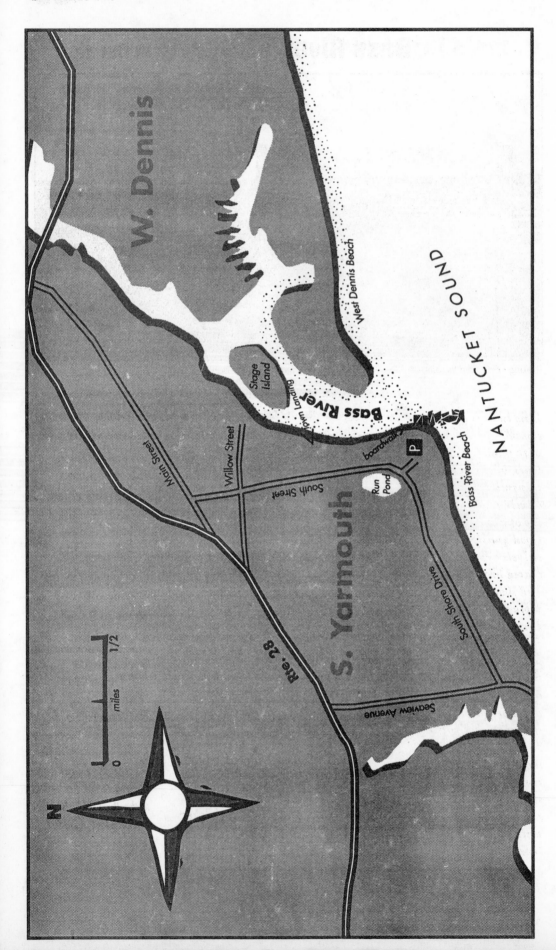

Bass River, Yarmouth/West Dennis

Looking north from the pier, into Bass River, West Dennis Beach is to the right.

Line twist is a common problem with monofilament lines, but it can be minimized or eliminated by the use of a snap swivel. Good quality snap swivels are made of coated brass or steel and should be replaced regularly. Use the smallest snap swivel possible so that the action of the lure won't be affected. Some lures are more prone to spinning and will twist the line in a short amount of time, while others swim in a side-to-side motion and are unlikely to cause line twist. And never, ever, reel

The entrance to **Bass River**, one of the largest tidal rivers on the Cape, surely must qualify as one of the most family-friendly places to fish on Cape Cod. A large parking area, picnic tables and a beach with life guards on duty in season gives the non-fishing members of the group plenty to do while the fishers pursue bluefish, stripers, fluke or scup off the jetty at the end of the river or from the large fishing pier.

This is not a place to expect a solitary fishing experience, but at times, especially when the bluefish are around, the action can be fast and furious. The southwest winds of summer push warm waters across the shallow sandflats at the river mouth, and the river itself is a huge baitfish nursery, guaranteeing a reliable food source for many different gamefishes. In fact, at the height of summer it's on this stretch of beach that exotic southern species are occasionally caught, fish like small jacks and banded runners, and even a wayward tarpon was once caught nearby.

Just about every fishing method will be effective in this location at one time or another during the season. Live or chunked herring account for some huge stripers off the jetty here in the spring, and live eels fished off the beach at night in the summer can be equally productive. Fly-

Directions:
Off of Route 28 in South Yarmouth, follow Main Street to South Street. Follow South Street, straight through the intersection of Willow Street, for 1 mile to the Bass River Beach parking lot on the left.

→   →

Bass River, Yarmouth/West Dennis
Continued

The riprap jetty extends from the boardwalk pier into Nantuket Sound.

against the drag when fighting a large fish with a spinning reel. This will put a twist in the line with every turn of the spool.

fishermen and light-tackle fans fish small jigs or flies that show a thin profile to imitate sand eels, an important forage in the shallow water near the beach. Bottom fishing off the pier, which is a safe and secure platform for fishing with small children, will produce scup and possibly black sea bass or fluke. Just be sure to get there early before the heavy boat traffic in the river puts the fish down for the day.

Adjacent to the beach and picnic area is a launching area with plenty of secure parking, a great place to launch a boat or perhaps a canoe or kayak to fish the marshy areas of the opposite shore. In fact, the entire river fishes well early or late in the day all summer, or at any time of day in the off season. Stripers can be caught all the way up past the Route 6 bridge, and the flats under that bridge are a great place to look for holdover stripers on a warm day in January. Bass River Beach is a wonderful place to introduce a youngster or novice to the fun of fishing.

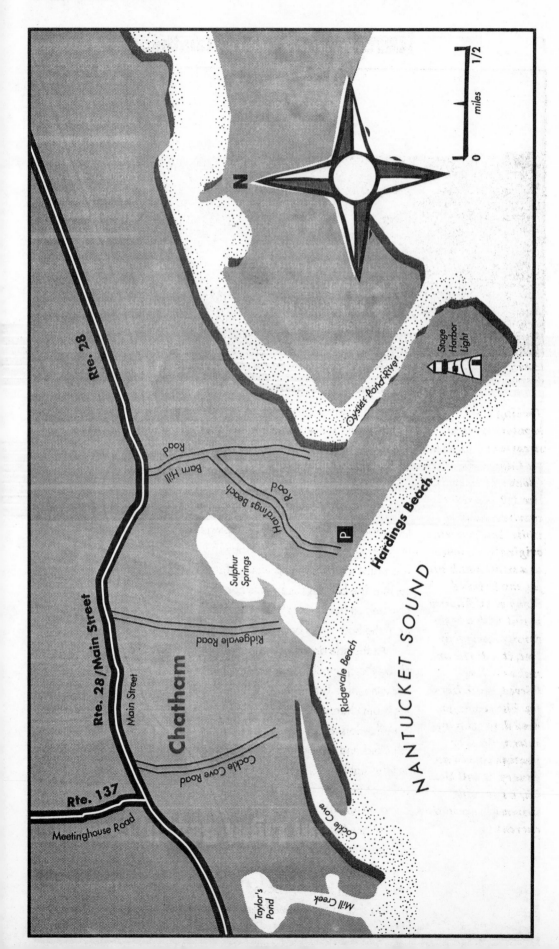

Hardings Beach, Chatham

Looking in a southeasterly direction along Hardings Beach, the angler can sometimes see Stage Harbor Light in the distance.

The single most popular saltwater streamer fly used on the Cape is the Clouser Minnow in size 1/0, colored chartreuse and white. This pattern, originally designed as a smallmouth bass fly, can be fished many ways. Allowed to sink with a high-density sinking fly line, it will rise and sink as it is retrieved, much like a jig. Fished using a dead drift with an intermediate or floating line in an estuary, it will look like a silverside swimming across the current.

With its shallow, gradually deepening sand bottom, sandbars with channels and scattered eelgrass patches, and prolific bait that's pushed in by the prevailing southwest wind, 1 1/2-mile **Hardings Beach** is popular with wading fishermen. The most important baitfish here are sand eels, which fill the waters from early June through September. On the southeastern end of the beach is Stage Harbor Light and the entrance to Stage Harbor. The channel entrance is quite a long walk from the parking lot, but is a prime spot with deep water and a fast current. The boat traffic here is heavy in the summer, so this area is best fished after dark or in the hour or so before dawn.

As the tide drops, sandbars are exposed along the channel edges. Fish the outflows between these bars where the flats empty into the main channel. Stripers will often be seen over the flats themselves. These fish are easily spooked and are quite challenging to catch, but the sight of a 20-pound fish cruising in two feet of water is sure to get any angler's heart pumping!

In late August and early September false albacore and bonito are caught off Hardings Beach, and sometimes they will charge in close enough for shore-bound anglers to have a shot at these speedsters.

Directions:
From the intersection of Routes 28 and 137, travel east for 1 1/2 miles on Route 28 to Barn Hill Road on the right. Follow Barn Hill Road for 1/2 mile to Harding's Beach Road on the right. Follow Harding's Beach Road to the parking area. Parking is available for a fee, with a sticker, at the beach from June 1 to September 1. The lot is open without charge all other months.

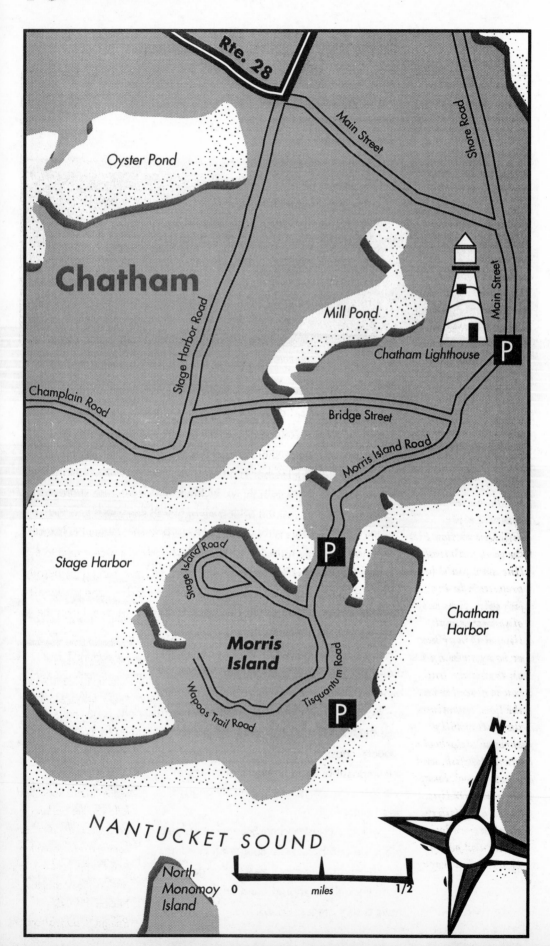

Morris Island, Chatham

North Monomoy Island is visible from Morris Island when looking toward the south.

A spare spool for your spinning reel is a good investment. It can save a day of fishing or allow you to adapt your equipment for different species. Fill the spool with fresh line, and you'll be prepared if a big fish takes away most of your original line, or if your lure or bait gets hung up on the bottom and you're forced to cut the line. Sometimes the angler will encounter a school of very large fish, and a spare spool, loaded with heavier line, may be the difference between losing tackle and going home with a trophy.

The southern tip of **Morris Island** is part of the Monomoy National Wildlife Refuge and, like Monomoy Island, offers some great fishing from its shores. Most locals agree that the fishing in the adjacent Chatham Harbor is not as good as it once was, before the new cut near Chatham Light. A 3/4-mile walk along the shore to the southerly tip of the island brings the angler to some very productive water however. This is the channel between Morris Island and North Monomoy Island, southeast of Hardings Beach. The water next to the beach is deep and fly-fishermen do very well here using high-density sinking lines in the fast current. A sandbar extends off the southwest corner of the island, and fish will wait for bait to be swept over the bar on a falling tide. As the tide drops, anglers will wade out on the bar and drift flies or lures over the edges. Be very careful wading here, particularly at times of extreme tides. The water can run so swiftly that sand can be pulled from beneath your wader boots, causing you to sink ever deeper, until it is impossible to move your feet.

Directions:

Take Route 28 to Main Street; follow Main Street east for 3/4 mile, then south for 1/3 mile past Chatham Light. Go left onto Morris Island Road and follow to the parking area along the dike, or continue on Tisquantum Road to the parking area at the Monomoy National Wildlife Refuge Headquarters.

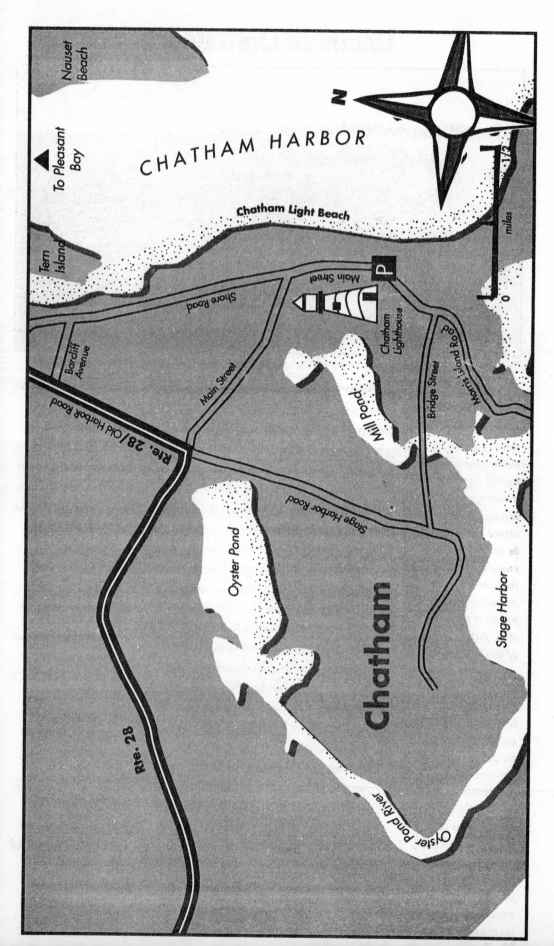

Chatham Light Beach, Chatham

The entrance to Pleasant Bay can be seen to the north from Chatham Light Beach.

To maximize casting distance potential with a spinning rod, the largest guide should have a diameter close to the diameter of the spool on the reel that will be used. Many custom-wrapped rods feature a large-diameter stripping guide of stainless steel, followed by a set of guides with ceramic or silicone carbide inserts. Conventional casting rods have smaller guides, but the largest should be the same height as the point that the line comes off a revolving spool. Regardless of the type of rod being used, select a rod that has four or more guides. This will insure that the line stays away from the

Four things distinguish **Chatham Light Beach**: easy access, plenty of parking, a beautiful location and consistently good fishing. This beach has changed radically in the last 20 years. At one time the sandy barrier that is Nauset Beach extended across the outlet in front of the light, and the south end of that beach was a legendary striped bass spot, accessible only by four-wheel-drive vehicle or boat. The cut in the barrier beach, which formed during a storm in the 1970s, changed the tidal flow from Pleasant Bay. Sand gradually built up along the beach to the right of the light and merged with the outer barrier beach. This is now called South Beach by the locals.

The channel forms quite close to the beach on the bend and is a great place to cast lures or flies or drift an eel after dark. An angler wading inside the Harbor to the north of the lighthouse beach will find shallower water where stripers feed after dark on sand eels. At the far end of the bend to the south, there are a series of sandbars extending off the corner of the inlet. These change on a year-to-year basis and are best explored in the daylight. Around this corner is the most southerly section of the Big Beach on Cape Cod. About two miles long, stripers and bluefish may be found anywhere along this outer beach. An energetic fisherman can walk to the end of this beach, and although this spot doesn't feature the legendary fishing of the days before the new cut, a nice rip still sets up here.

Directions:
Take Route 28 into Chatham, onto Main Street. Follow Main Street east, then south to the parking area.

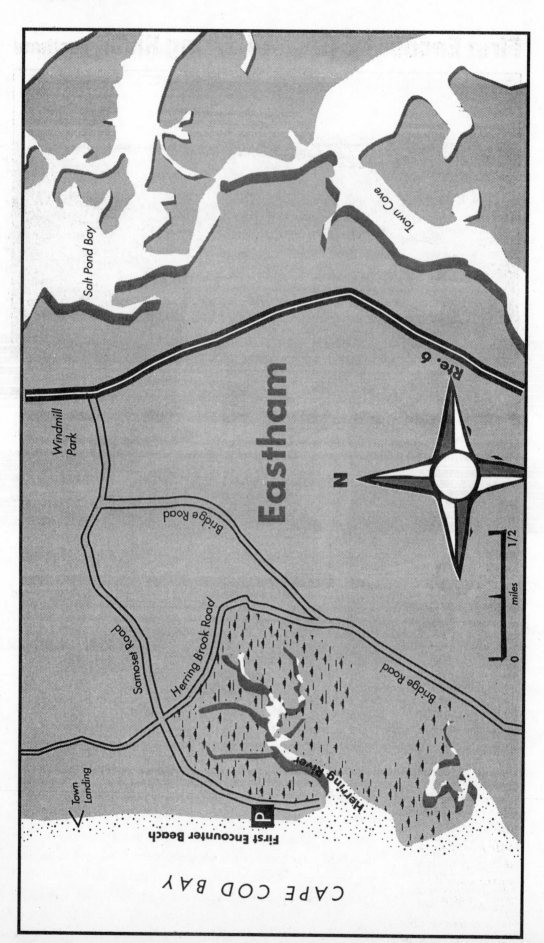

First Encounter Beach/Herring River, Eastham

The channel of Herring River, looking west toward Cape Cod Bay.

Scouting out potential fishing spots at low tide will help the fisherman make an educated guess as to where the fish will be at high tide. Structure such as boulders, old riprap, and the remains of piers and jetties hold bait and attract predators, but they're often hard to see at a higher stage of the tide. On the outer beaches, deep channels between sandbars are the highways used by stripers and bluefish. Savvy anglers find these channels at low tide and line them up with a landmark on shore to find them again when the water is deep.

First Encounter Beach, named for the first (unhappy) encounter between the Pilgrims and the local Native American inhabitants in 1620 near this spot, has good fish-holding potential. This is because of the cover offered by grass patches just offshore and the marsh behind the beach that flushes bait out into Cape Cod Bay through **Herring River** with each falling tide. This is a very popular bathing beach and can get quite crowded on a typical summer afternoon, so the wise fisherman will work this beach at night or in the predawn hours.

Local fishermen will wade out with the dropping tide to rake sand eels from the shallows with long-tined rakes designed for this purpose, then return as the tide is flooding and fish this fresh bait on the bottom. Another popular method here is to walk and cast toward the grass patches just off the beach with flies or plugs. Stripers will often congregate in or near these darker patches of water, and if one patch does not produce, keep walking and casting until you find one that does.

Directions:
From Route 6 in Eastham center, go west 1.8 miles on Samoset Road to the parking area.

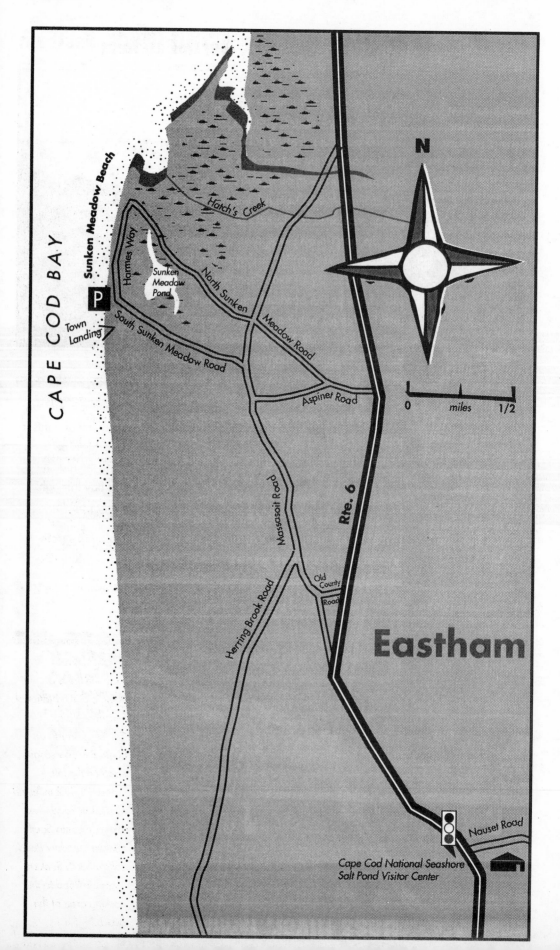

CAPE COD BAY

Sunken Meadow Beach

Hatch's Creek

Harmes Way

Sunken Meadow Pond

North Sunken

Meadow Road

P

Town Landing

South Sunken Meadow Road

Aspinet Road

N

0   miles   1/2

Massasoit Road

Rte. 6

Herring Brook Road

Old County Road

Eastham

Nauset Road

Cape Cod National Seashore
Salt Pond Visitor Center

Sunken Meadow Beach, North Eastham

Sunken Meadow Beach stretches to the north from the parking area.

Experienced Cape fishermen know that nighttime is the right time for striped bass in the summer months. Spots that seem devoid of sea life will come alive when the sun goes down. Cooling water and the cover of darkness makes stripers much less wary, and often they will feed almost at the angler's feet. It's important that the fisherman use all his senses when fishing after dark and when visibility is limited. The sound of feeding stripers is distinctive, giving hints of what the bass are eating. A soft, deliberate, slurping sound usually indicates the presence of small baits, like silversides, sand eels or worms. A splashy, loud rise signals that the fish are chasing large baitfish, such as pogies, herring or squid.

Sunken Meadow Beach in North Eastham fishes well early and late in the season and is a favorite with bait fishermen. The first keeper-sized striper caught on this side of the Cape often comes from this beach. Early season fishermen prefer fresh chunk bait, such as herring and mackerel. It's common to see anglers raking sand eels at low tide, then returning two hours before high tide and fishing with their fresh bait. In the late season, a moderate onshore breeze from the north will push bait up against the beach and big stripers will follow.

Directions:

From the lights on Route 6 at the National Seashore Visitor Center, go north on Route 6 to Massasoit Road on the left. Proceed 1 1/2 miles on Massasoit Road, then take a left onto South Sunken Meadow Road. Follow South Sunken Meadow Road to the parking area at the beach.

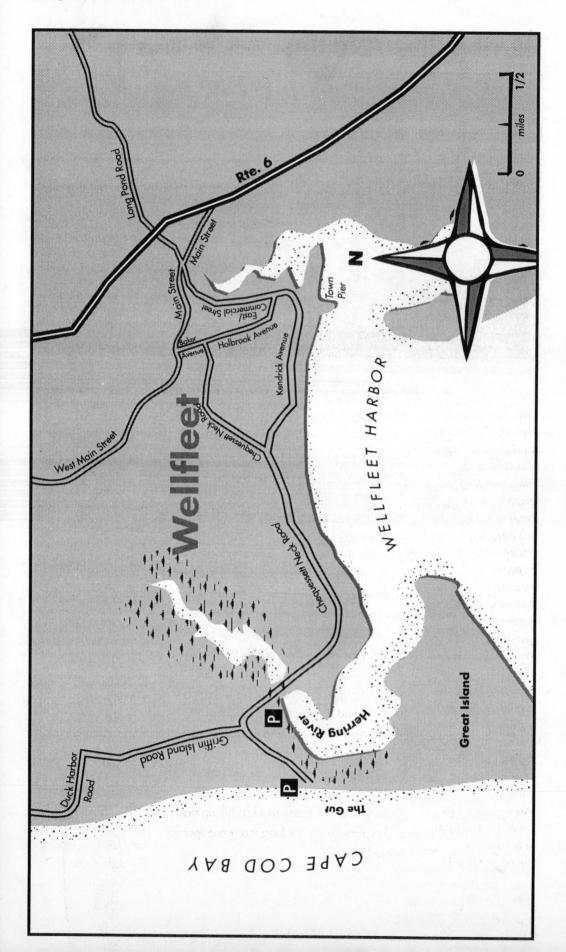

Herring River/Great Island, **Wellfleet**

Looking south from Herring River, toward Wellfleet Harbor, Great Island is to the far right.

Pilot whales feed over the shallows and sand flats of Cape Cod Bay, and sometimes they get trapped by the dropping tide. When this happens, a whale rescue network responds, and volunteers work to save as many of the mammals as possible, herding the stronger whales back out to sea. But this was not always the way Cape Codders responded to a whale stranding. In the eighteenth and nineteenth centuries a whale on the beach was seen as a gift from the Almighty, to be eaten or rendered for oil.

Herring River empties into the northwest end of Wellfleet Harbor and is a very productive location for fishermen using live or chunk herring in the spring and swimming plugs in the fall. The edge of the marsh, where the river opens into the harbor, is preferred by fly-fishermen. Schoolie stripers are caught along these edges in the summer at night, and, occasionally, bluefish will push bait right up to the river outflow below the dike.

Over the hill, beyond the dike, is **Great Island**, part of the Cape Cod National Seashore. The Bayside beachfront at the end of the paved road is called the Gut and is one of most consistently productive locations on Cape Cod Bay. This is probably due to a rocky shore, a consistent supply of bait in the form of sand eels and good tidal flow. All fishing methods work here, from plugging to bait fishing to fly-fishing. As with most locations on the Bay side, an onshore wind and the top part of the tide is preferred. Great Island has many marked hiking trails and a picnic area, making it a great spot for a family outing.

Directions:
Follow Route 6 to Main Street. Bear left onto East Commercial Street, which merges into Commercial Street. Bear right at the town pier onto Kendrick Avenue. Kendrick merges with Chequessett Neck Road. Follow Chequessett for 1 1/2 miles to the dike over Herring River. Park near the dike (off the pavement) in the spring and fall, or drive over the dike, up the hill, to the picnic area.

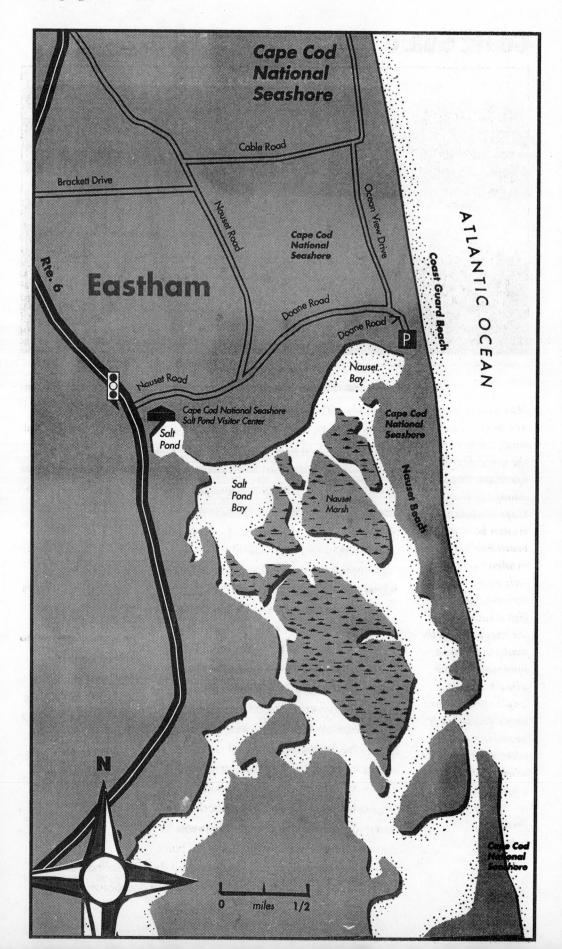

Coast Guard Beach/Nauset Inlet, Eastham

Looking east from the Doane Road parking area, the Atlantic Ocean crashes onto Coast Guard Beach.

Many large stripers are caught in the wash, the area where the waves break against the beach. Along the Outer Cape beaches a deep trough between the beach and the first sandbar holds small bait and cruising stripers. Be sure to fish a lure or fly all the way through the wash, as fish will sometimes follow almost to the angler's feet before they strike. This is particularly true after dark or on days when the surf is high.

The only thing more spectacular than the fishing along **Coast Guard Beach** is the scenery. Looking south from the parking lot at the old Coast Guard station, the barrier beach and Nauset Marsh stretch out for three miles to the entrance of **Nauset Inlet**. A series of sandbars mark the entrance of the inlet and anglers will often plan an entire day or night of fishing around the walk from the parking area to the bars.

Stripers and bluefish can be found anywhere along this shore, and every deep hole and cut between the sandbars should be explored. There is a deep trough along most of the beach that stripers use as a highway between the beach itself and the outer bar. Often fish will be caught in the wash of the first wave at the angler's feet. Plug fishing is effective here, as is swimming a live eel after dark in the fall. Fly-fishermen should use weighted lines and flies, and be sure to keep solid contact with the fly as they retrieve.

At the far end of the beach is the entrance to the Inlet. This deep channel can hold very large stripers after dark. A series of bars extends off the end of the beach at the mouth of the inlet. The channels between these bars are concentration points for bait and stripers. Be aware that the forces that shape these bars and channels, strong current in and out of the inlet and ocean surf, make this a location for experienced waders only.

Directions:

From the traffic lights on Route 6 at the Cape Cod National Seashore Visitor Center, follow Nauset Road east onto Doane Road, to the parking area at Coast Guard Beach.

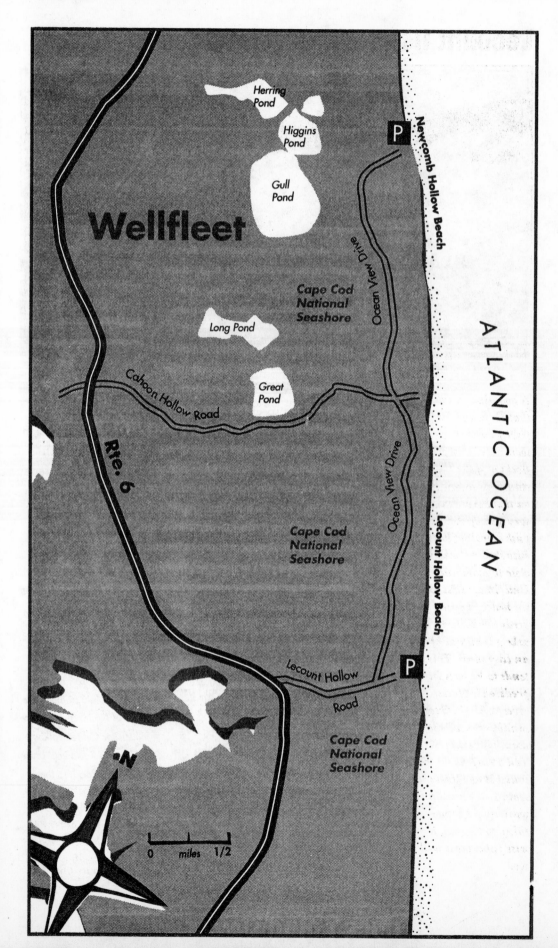

Lecount Hollow/Newcomb Hollow, Wellfleet

The view from the parking area at the end of Lecount Hollow Road looks across Lecount Hollow Beach to the Atlantic.

A good indicator that there was just fishing action, or soon will be, are flocks of gulls standing in one area on the shore. Predatory gamefish will push schools of bait into shallow water close to shore and sometimes right onto the beach. The sea birds are there to take advantage of an easy meal. This tends to happen in predicable places; coves, bowls between sandbars, near the mouths of estuaries and outlets to marshes are likely spots. If the gulls are waiting for something to happen, a wise fisherman will too.

Lecount Hollow Beach and **Newcomb Hollow Beach** are typical of the outer Cape's east side. They begin fishing well in the first part of June and all methods will catch fish here, including chunk-bait fishing with herring in the early season, sand eels on the bottom in midseason, live eels after dark in September and October, and lures or flies anytime. Scout these beaches in the daytime at low tide to find the cuts between the outer sandbars, then return and fish these cuts on the incoming tide after dark or at first light for big striped bass.

As with all the beaches in the National Seashore on what's known as the Backside, fishing is dependent on surf and wind conditions. A light to moderate onshore breeze is preferred, but unfortunately this wind often pushes in a seaweed called mung, which makes fishing impossible. Before planning a fishing trip to the Outer Cape beaches, a prudent angler will call one of the local tackle shops to find out if the water is "dirty."

Directions:
Off Route 6 in Wellfleet, follow Lecount Hollow Road 1 mile to the beach. Or bear left onto Ocean View Drive at the entrance of Lecount Hollow Beach; follow Ocean View Drive for 3 miles to Newcomb Hollow Beach.

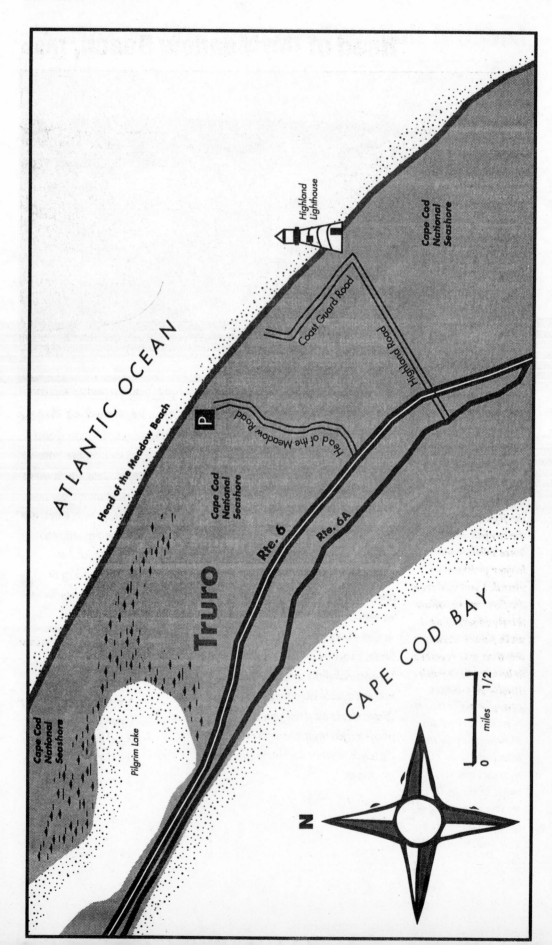

Head of the Meadow Beach, Truro

The remains of a sunken boat can be seen from Head of the Meadow Beach.

Weighted fly lines, 250 to 350 grains, are popular with anglers along the Outer Cape beaches. This heavy line gets the fly down below the surface turbulence where the larger fish are found. Cast out over the first wave, allow the fly to settle, and walk slowly backward as you retrieve to be sure that you're always in contact with the fly.

Located within the Cape Cod National Seashore, **Head of the Meadow Beach** is similar to High Head to the north and Coast Guard (Truro) to the south. There are fewer sandbars offshore here compared with the beaches in Eastham and Orleans, and deep water can be found just off the beach.

Although anglers will find bass and bluefish along these beaches starting in late May, this area really comes into its own in September and October. Many fishermen prefer the first three hours of the incoming tide here, using sand eels or cut bait such as herring or menhaden. If the surf is running high, try metal lures to get below the waves.

In years past hearty fishermen would fish these beaches in the winter months after dark for cod. Casting a live eel or a plug into the surf on a cool autumn night can produce the striped bass of a lifetime, and for many people, fishing these wild, windswept beaches is what surf fishing on Cape Cod is all about.

Directions:

From Route 6 in Truro, head northeast on Head of the Meadow Road for one mile to the parking area.

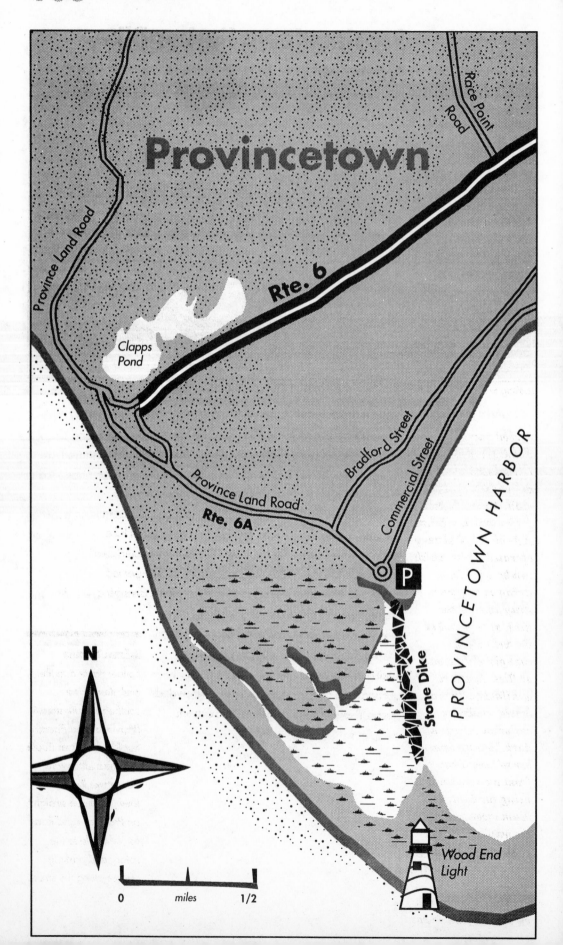

Provincetown Harbor Dike,
Provincetown

Looking to the south from the Stone Dike, Wood End Light is visible in the distance.

A good quality flashlight is an indispensable tool for the wading fisherman. Many anglers prefer the aluminum, AA- or AAA-battery-operated lights, which can be worn on a string or clipped on a strap around the neck, then placed in the teeth while changing lures, bait or flies. Some are available with red lenses, which are easier on the eyes after dark. Always remember to turn away from the water when using the light, as a beam shooting over the water will spook cruising and feeding fish. For this reason, it's good to avoid headlamps that strap on the forehead or hat.

The **Provincetown Harbor Dike** on the inner part of the harbor stretches out from the end of the village toward Wood End and Long Point. This mile-long, man-made structure is a great destination for anglers who enjoy bottom fishing or families with younger members. Access is easy and there's plenty of room to fish. Fluke, stripers and bluefish are caught here in the summer, and sand eels are by far the most popular bait. The period from two hours before, up to high tide is best. Energetic fishermen will make the long walk down the length of the dike to the outer beaches from Wood End Light down to Long Point for outstanding beach fishing. The relative remoteness of this beach ensures uncrowded fishing, even at the height of the summer.

Directions:
Follow Route 6 to the end; then drive southeast on Route 6A (Province Land Road) for 1 mile. When Route 6A turns left toward downtown Province-town, continue straight on Province Land Road for 1/4 mile to the rotary and parking spaces along the street.

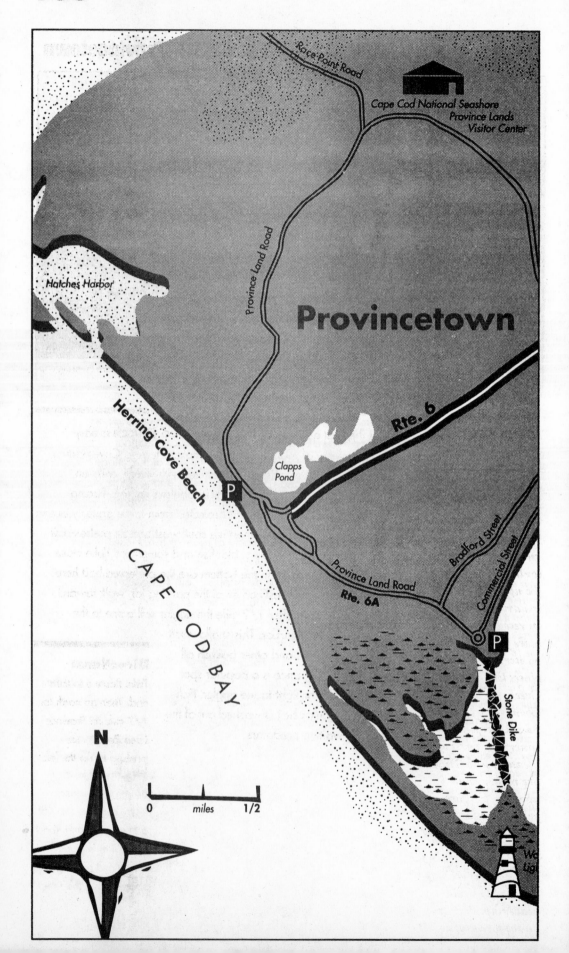

Cape Cod National Seashore
Province Lands
Visitor Center

Race Point Road

Province Land Road

Provincetown

Hatches Harbor

Rte. 6

Clapps Pond

Herring Cove Beach

P

Bradford Street

Commercial Street

Province Land Road

Rte. 6A

P

CAPE COD BAY

Stone Dike

N

0   miles   1/2

Wo
Ligh

Herring Cove Beach, Provincetown

From the parking area an angler can look along Herring Cove Beach toward Hatches Harbor and Race Point Light to the northwest.

Fishing for holdover striped bass has become very popular in recent years. Although long-time Cape fishermen have always known that an occasional striper could be caught in the upper reaches of estuaries and bays, in recent years many more fish are wintering-over in places like Scorton Creek, the Coonamessett River, Bass River and the innermost parts of Pleasant Bay. These are mostly small schoolies, but they provide a nice diversion for fishermen with cabin fever in the dead of winter.

One of the best qualities of **Herring Cove Beach** is easy access and plenty of room to fish. This makes Herring Cove particularly attractive to elderly fishers or families with young children.

The other attraction of the beach is fabulous fishing. Facing southwest, the beach is somewhat protected from large easterly ocean swells, but the prevailing summertime southwest breeze pushes bait close to the beach with stripers, bluefish and sometimes fluke close behind. Sand eels fished on the bottom are the preferred bait here.

From the far northwest corner of the parking lot, walk toward Race Point Light, and after 1/2 mile the angler will come to the entrance to Hatches Harbor. This shallow salt pond holds sand eels and other baitfish all season, and the entrance is a popular spot for the fly-rodder or light-tackle angler. Fish the dropping tide as bait is washed out of the salt pond to waiting predators.

Directions:
Take Route 6 to the end. Then go north for 1/2 mile on Province Land Road to the parking lot on the left.

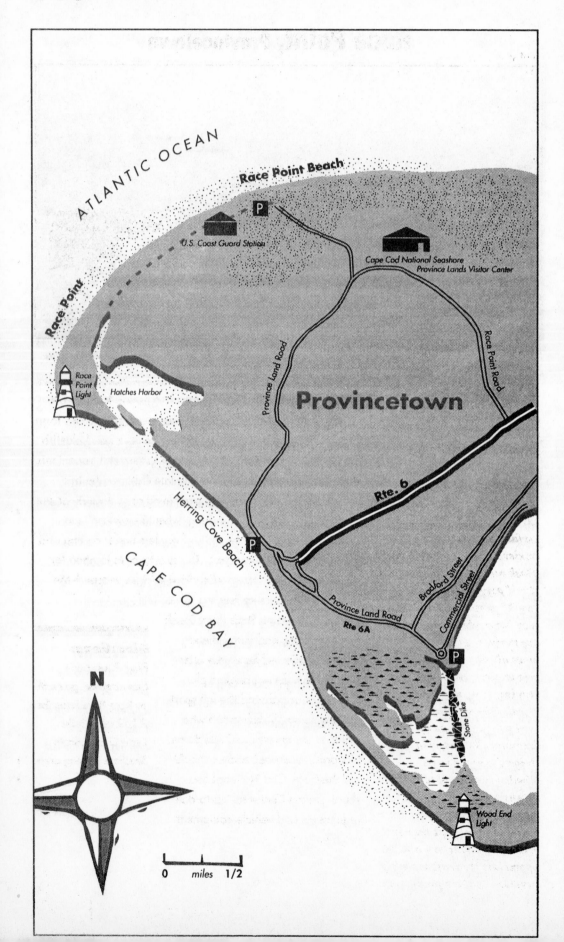

Race Point, Provincetown

Large boats close to shore are indicative of deep water well within casting range.

Wooden plugs continue to be the most popular type of lure fished on the Cape, from the Canal to the big surf beaches of the outer Cape. Many of these lures were developed on the Cape for fishing under a variety of conditions. Some surface plugs are made to be retrieved quickly with lots of splash and motion. Some, like pencil poppers, are made to "walk" across the surface with very little splash, and some are surface swimmers, which move along with a side-to-side motion, much like a herring or menhaden. Needlefish-type plugs, fished very slowly after dark, have accounted for many large stripers over the years. Wooden lures tend to be more expensive than their plastic cousins, but most experienced surfcasters feel that they are better fish attractors, and they appreciate the craftsmanship involved in their production.

Race Point is the most famous surf-fishing location on Cape Cod for good reason. Currents converge and rips form just off the beach, and many trophy-sized bass and bluefish are caught here every year. Although fishermen frequent this area from the end of May through late October, the best fishing takes place in the fall. Swimming or surface plugs are effective, as is chunk bait fishing, when the surf isn't too severe, but most experienced surf anglers prefer casting and retrieving live eels after dark. This is a favorite location for fishermen who use four-wheel-drive vehicles to search the beachfront for surface feeding fish. The bass blitzes on Race Point Beach are legendary, and many friendships are renewed here year after year, as out-of-town anglers plan their vacations around the fall sportfish migrations. A fisherman who wants to use an off-road vehicle on National Seashore beaches should call the Cape Cod National Seashore Visitors Center for up-to-date regulations and vehicle equipment requirements.

Directions:

From Route 6 in Provincetown, go north on Race Point Road for 2 1/2 miles to the Cape Cod National Seashore parking area.

Notes:

Notes:

Notes: